The Metaphysician in the Dark

D1562940

POETS ON POETRY

David Lehman, General Editor
Donald Hall, Founding Editor

New titles

Thomas M. Disch, *The Castle of Perseverance*
Mark Jarman, *Body and Soul*
Philip Levine, *So Ask*
David Mura, *Song for Uncle Tom, Tonto, and Mr. Moto*
Karl Shapiro, *Essay on Rime*
Charles Simic, *The Metaphysician in the Dark*
Stephen Yenser, *A Boundless Field*

Recently published

Tess Gallagher, *Soul Barnacles*
Linda Gregerson, *Negative Capability*
Philip Levine, *The Bread of Time*
Larry Levis, *The Gazer Within*
William Matthews, *The Poetry Blues*
Charles Simic, *A Fly in the Soup*

Also available are collections by

A. R. Ammons, Robert Bly, Philip Booth, Marianne Boruch,
Hayden Carruth, Fred Chappell, Amy Clampitt, Tom Clark,
Douglas Crase, Robert Creeley, Donald Davie, Peter Davison,
Tess Gallagher, Suzanne Gardinier, Allen Grossman, Thom Gunn,
Rachel Hadas, John Haines, Donald Hall, Joy Harjo, Robert Hayden,
Edward Hirsch, Daniel Hoffman, Jonathan Holden, John Hollander,
Andrew Hudgins, Josephine Jacobsen, Weldon Kees, Galway Kinnell,
Mary Kinzie, Kenneth Koch, John Koethe, Yusef Komunyakaa,
Richard Kostelanetz, Maxine Kumin, Martin Lammon (editor),
Philip Larkin, David Lehman, Philip Levine, John Logan,
William Logan, William Matthews, William Meredith, Jane Miller,
Carol Muske, Geoffrey O'Brien, Gregory Orr, Alicia Suskin Ostriker,
Ron Padgett, Marge Piercy, Anne Sexton, Charles Simic,
Louis Simpson, William Stafford, Anne Stevenson, May Swenson,
James Tate, Richard Tillinghast, Diane Wakoski, C. K. Williams,
Alan Williamson, Charles Wright, and James Wright

Charles Simic

The Metaphysician in the Dark

Ann Arbor

THE UNIVERSITY OF MICHIGAN PRESS

A CIP catalog record for this book is available from the British Library.

Library of Congress Cataloging-in-Publication Data

Simic, Charles, 1938–
    The metaphysician in the dark / Charles Simic.
        p. cm. — (Poets on poetry)
    ISBN 0-472-09830-6 (cloth : alk. paper) — ISBN 0-472-06830-X
(pbk. : alk. paper)
        1. Simic, Charles, 1938—Aesthetics.   2. Poetry—Authorship.
3. Poetry.   I. Title.   II. Series.
PS3569.I4725   Z469   2003
811'.54—dc21
                                                        2002153620

Contents

In Praise of Folly

> Folly is in poor repute
> even among the greatest fools.
> —Erasmus

1

It's almost the year 2000. All the New York City hotel rooms and fine restaurants are already booked for New Year's Eve. The astrologers are busy predicting the future, and so are the Pentagon and the CIA. Ancient Babylonian princesses and Egyptian priests are sending daily messages through the mouths of housewives in Texas and New Jersey. Many strange occurrences are due to take place, we are told weekly in supermarket tabloids: A huge monument to Elvis Presley will be sighted on Mars. Doctors will bring Abraham Lincoln back to life for ninety-nine seconds. Vintage red wines will be made from plastic cups discarded in fast-food restaurants. With a single wire inserted in the ear, we'll be able to tape our dreams the way we tape TV programs on our VCR.

But what about poetry? What will the poets be doing in the next century? You do not have to be a Nostradamus to predict that the poets will be doing exactly what they've been doing for the last three thousand years: howling and kicking about how nobody ever appreciates them.

Here is a thought I had recently while strolling in New York. Out of the blue, so to speak, I remembered Sappho. I had spent the afternoon in a bookstore turning the pages of new books of poetry, and it suddenly occurred to me that if she were miraculously to come back from the dead and were to see this crowd

---

From *Georgia Review* 52, no. 4 (winter 1998).

and this traffic, she'd of course be terrified, but if a few of the contemporary lyric poems I had just read were translated for her, she'd be on familiar ground. Astonishing! I thought. I'm an almost three-thousand-year-old poet, and didn't know it! The kind of poetry I write today has its origins in what she started doing back then.

Here then is the story of my life:

When I was still a snot-nosed kid, my name was Ovid, Horace, Catullus, Sextus Propertius, and Martial. My specialty was mixing the serious with the trivial, the frivolous with the highminded. I was a holy terror. I wrote lines like these:

> When she's on her chaise-long,
> Make haste to find a footstool
> For those dainty feet of hers,
> Help her on and off with the slippers.

"Better a metropolitan city were sacked," Robert Burton wrote, "a royal army overcome, an invincible armada sunk and twenty thousand kings should perish, than her little finger ache." That was my plan, too. I had nothing to do with sundry windbags who wrote odes to every two-bit tyrant who came along, tabulated their conquests, glorified their slaughter of the barbarians, and praised their incomparable wisdom in peace and war. I poked fun at the rich and the powerful, gossiping about their wives and daughters milking cocks while their husbands' and daddies' backs were turned. I didn't even spare the gods. I turned them into a lot of brawling, drunken, revengeful, senile wife swappers.

I myself roamed the streets of Rome frequently inebriated. I fell in and out of love a thousand times, never failing to tell the whole world about my new love's incomparable virtues and perversities. Then, I got into trouble. The emperor packed me off to permanent exile in a godforsaken hellhole at the farthest reaches of the empire. His guardians of virtue took the opportunity to warn the populace against lyric poetry—which is nothing more, they said, than a call to debauchery and a brazen mockery of everything ever held sacred.

Of course, nobody bothered the official eulogists-for-hire,

who were busy protecting the solemnities of state and church from ridicule. It was the lyric poem, with its exaltation of intimacy, that had been suspect ever since Sappho started the craze by elevating individual destiny over the fate of the tribe, preferring to savor Anactoria"s "lovely step, her sparkling glance and her face," rather than "gaze on all the troops in Lydia in their chariots and glittering armor."

It's true. It was the love of that kind of irreverence, as much as anything else, that started me in poetry. The itch to make fun of authority, to break taboos, to celebrate the naked body, to claim that one has seen an angel in the same breath as one shouts that there's no God, and so forth. The discovery that the tragic and the comic are always entwined made me roll on the floor with happiness. Seduction, too, was always on my mind: if you take off your shirt, my love, and let my tongue get acquainted with yours, I'll praise your beauty in my poems and your name will live forever. It worked, too. Much of lyric poetry is nothing more than a huge, centuries-old effort to remind our immortal souls of the existence of our genital organs.

In the so-called Dark Ages, when mud was everywhere up to the knees, the common folk made their bed for the night on the dirt floor, cozy and blissful in one big embrace with their pigs and sheep; hens perched on the rafters over their heads; and only the dogs slept with one of their eyes open, on the lookout for roaming poets. For centuries, not only yokels but also ladies and gents had little to amuse themselves with but a few strains of Gregorian chant and the daily earful of a lot of bad cussing about the hard life and the weather. I was a lone, bummed-out, lice-ridden monk, reduced to roving the countryside and begging every night for a few crumbs and a bit of straw to sleep on in some rich man's drafty castle. There, in gratitude for the hospitality, I would offer a gamut of racy love poems, pious legends of saints' lives, drinking songs, funeral laments, faithful-wife poems, and sly satires on the way of kings and popes. At the same time, I had to be extra careful to make the murderous and drunken company at the table laugh and even shed a tear at how hungry and cold, how skinny and forlorn I looked now that—*oh the sweet voice of the woodland nightingale*—I'd even lost my cloak and breeches at dice!

I turn to you in misery and tears
As turns the stag, when his strength gives out.

You get the idea? Oh, the guises I had—more aliases than all the con artists of the world put together. I was that petty felon Villon, who almost ended up strung by his neck; Guillem IX, Duke of Aquitaine, who wrote his poems while he snored away in the saddle; Shakespeare, who some scholars tell you was not really called that but something else; Signor Dante, who gave us a first-class tour of hell to prepare us for the horrors of the twentieth century; and so many others. My fondest incarnation remains Thomas Bastard, who lived from 1566 to 1618 and whose life and career my anthology of Elizabethan verse describes, more or less, thus:

A country clergyman who made pitiably small headway in life, Bastard published his book in 1598. It was much ridiculed. Bastard died, touched in his wits, in debtors' prison in Dorcester.

My life was like the history of costumes. One season I wore a powdered wig, rode in a glass coach, and scribbled sonnets on the cuff of my shirt between duels, taking time out to praise classical measures and restraint; next I was a wild-haired revolutionary shouting encouragement to the crowd while standing on some real or imaginary barricade, assuring my listeners that we poets are nothing less than the unacknowledged legislators of the world.

Some nerve, you must be saying to yourself. Ha-ha! Just wait till I tell you about my American adventures.

2

No sooner had Columbus sailed back to Spain than I started scribbling poems. It must have been the climate in the New World—hot and humid in the south, bleak and cold in the north—that for years kept me from getting a decent poem written in this vast land of mystery. How many still remember that the first explorers and settlers expected to run into the Chinese over the next horizon? The Frenchman Nicollet even went and provided himself in Paris with a robe of Chinese damask embroidered with birds and flowers, in order to be properly attired while crossing the prairie and finally sitting down to sip tea and schmooze with some old mandarin. In any case, it took me years of sleepwalking before I could open my eyes and see where I truly was.

Forget about El Dorado and New Jerusalem. Forget about the devil in the forest and the comely witches stripping to frolic naked around his campfire. Forget about Oriental spices and jewels. Here were grim little towns with factory walls blackened by age. Here were crowded tenements with men and women huddled against the weather, lying on their sides, knees drawn up, their heads touching the roach-infested floor. Here were seedy rooming houses populated by an assortment of loners, eccentrics, bad poets, and a dozen other kinds of losers.

How quickly the New World got old for me. Some days it felt like being buried alive. I was weary, resigned like Bartleby to staring at walls. Yet on other days the windows were wide open, the sun was shining, America still remained to be truly discovered.

The poet is the eye and tongue of every living and every inanimate thing, I told everyone I met. Poetry is nothing less than a divinely appointed medium. God himself doesn't speak prose, but communicates with us through hints, omens, and not-yet-perceived resemblances in objects lying around us. Unfortunately, American life storms about us daily, but is slow to find a tongue. I looked in vain, I shouted like a street preacher, for the poet whom I describe.

It didn't take long. I grew a white beard and made the announcement that Americans, of all people at any time upon the earth, have probably the fullest poetical nature, and that the United States themselves are essentially the greatest poem.

How do you like that? I said to myself.

This is what you shall do, I wrote. Love the earth, the sun, and the animals, despise riches, give alms to everyone who asks, stand up for the stupid and crazy, reexamine everything you have been told in school and church or any book, hate tyrants, and dismiss whatever insults your soul. Do these things, and your very flesh shall be a great poem.

I tell you, I felt right at home in America.

All truths wait in all things to be discovered, I proclaimed. The number of unknown heroes is equal to the number of greatest heroes known, and I will name them all. The cow with its head bowed and munching the grass surpasses any statue.

I went on to make a poem of things overlooked, slighted, and forbidden. Still and all, my exuberant praise of all matters sexual was a permanent scandal in a country founded by the followers of Calvin.

At the very same time I was saying all that, however, I had a secret other, someone reserved and suspicious in the face of my utopian grandeur and self-confident rhetoric. We live in a magic prison, a haunted house, a dark labyrinth, an inscrutable forest, my other said; we are trapped in a finite infinite, an uncertain certainty, caught in a maze of oxymorons and paradoxes in a universe whose chief characteristic is its ambiguity. That other America came with a large graveyard. In it, the poet is a recluse, a secret blasphemer, and a heroic failure at best.

What my two sides had in common was an inability to submit to bounds and limits. They both aimed to join heaven and earth in their poems. What an ideal pickle to find oneself in, especially as an immigrant: Poetry as the place where fundamental epistemological, metaphysical, and aesthetic questions can be raised and answered. Poetry as the process through which ideas are tested, dramatized, made both a personal and a cosmic issue. I liked that. The poet's struggle may be solitary, but it is an exemplary struggle nevertheless.

American poetry's dizzying ambition to answer all the major philosophical and theological questions is unparalleled. Grand inquisitors, philosopher kings, totalitarian cops of all stripes would have plenty to do with me after a pronouncement like the following: "The poet—when he is writing—is a priest; the poem is a temple; epiphanies and communion take place within it."

Spiritual adventurer is the name of the game, folks. In America I bragged that I was starting from scratch, naked, without history and often without any religious belief, climbing an imaginary ladder up to heaven to find out for myself what all the fuss is about. I made American literature into a great paradox factory. On one hand, I desired to embody and express rare visionary states, and on the other, I wished to give my readers a hard and dry look at everyday reality. Literalists of the imagination—that's what I wanted us to be. Finding a place for the genuine in this artifice we call poetry (which I myself admitted disliking) was my great project. My most original achievement may very well have been my odd insistence that the only way to tell human beings about angels is to show them a blade of grass.

3

Ah, the three-thousand-year-old poet! You've got to see the nightmares I get from all the bad poems I've written. A day doesn't go by without some professor wagging her finger at me. Why, only recently I was described as a self-pitying little fascist, peddling his phallocentric, petit bourgeois claptrap. Twenty centuries of ridicule, my friends! Pedants poring over my poems, then teaching them to the young in such a way that the children are guaranteed to hate poetry for the rest of their lives. Some mornings, when the weather is damp, I get a sore neck, as if I were still Sir Walter Raleigh, convicted on charges of blasphemy and sedition, awaiting the executioner's ax in the Tower of London.

Here's my view of these long centuries:

One century's no worse than the other, if you ask me. A break in the clouds once in a while, an afternoon nap in the shade in the arms of your one and only, maybe a kiss or two, and that's about it. Sooner or later, the meal gets eaten, and we're left with just some chicken bones on our plate. The rest of the time it's plagues, wars, famines, persecutions, exile, and hundreds of other calamities and miseries that rule the day.

I suppose, dear readers, you think I am exaggerating? You imagine yourselves, of course, in a palazzo attended and closely fussed over by numerous servants while you argue with princes and highborn floozies about the paintings of Titian and the metaphysics of Campanella's *City of the Sun*. Don't make me laugh. All I see is open sewers in a street, reeking with the stench of horse and human excrement, while nearby a twelve-year-old witch is being burned at the stake by the Inquisition.

The true poets always know the score. Happiness, love, and the vision of the Almighty and his angels come and go. The moment we taste a morsel of bliss, begin to savor it and lick our lips—oops! Our house catches fire, someone runs off with our wife, or we break our leg. Poetry is best, therefore, when it finds itself at the heart of the human comedy; there's no more reliable reporter of what it means to be in this pickle. My view is that poetry is inevitable, irreplaceable, and necessary as daily bread. Even if we were to find ourselves living in the crummiest country in the world, in an age of unparalleled vileness and stupidity, we'd find that poetry still got written.

I know what troubles you: all the hyperbole poets are prone to, all that monkey talk and bizarre imagery we are forever hustling. Poets allege that the only way to tell the truth is to lie plenty. They put trust in their metaphors and in their wildest flights of the imagination. Poetry, they argue, is the only place where an incorrigible liar can have an honest existence, providing he or she lies really well.

My dear reader, *don't you see?*

Life would be perfectly pointless if I, the poet, didn't come and tell you—in so many ingenious ways—that all your amours, all your secret sufferings and fond memories, are potentially significant, deeply important, and even intelligible, and that you, when all's said and done, dear reader, really have no cause to fret about anything, as long as I'm here, night and day, doing the worrying for you.

The Devil Is a Poet

Last May, on my first trip to Lisbon, I finally had the opportunity to see Bosch's *Temptation of St. Anthony*. On a rainy weekday morning, the Museu Nacional de Arte Antigua, a converted seventeenth-century palace, appeared closed. After my friend and I paid the admission in the dim lobby, we encountered no one, except for an occasional guard dozing off on his or her feet. It was so quiet in the museum that every time we stopped before a painting, we could hear ourselves breathe. The palace houses the largest collection of fifteenth- and sixteenth-century Portuguese paintings in the world, muddy with age and badly in need of cleaning. We made our lengthy tour among what were mostly religious paintings, admiring a few works here and there, lingering for a while in the applied-arts wing before the marvelous Japanese screen showing a Portuguese delegation disembarking in Nagasaki in the sixteenth century, but finally we had to ask one of the women attendants as to the whereabouts of Bosch.

We crossed several cavernous rooms, the martyrs being tormented in the paintings seemingly as surprised by our sudden appearance as we were by theirs, and just as we began to suspect that we had misunderstood the directions we were given, there was the altarpiece, far larger than we had expected it to be. The triptych was set up and slightly elevated on a kind of platform, well lit, newly cleaned, its reds, blues, and yellows bright and rich, the details vivid, the whole spectacle simply breathtaking. For a painting to still be able to shock after almost five centuries is no small accomplishment. How many other works of art can do that? We stood before it absolutely stunned, overwhelmed

From *Tin House* 1, no. 3 (winter 2000).

and supremely happy, thinking, There cannot be any other world but this. Surprisingly, all that feverish activity, with its myriad of grotesque particulars in all three panels, gave the impression of coherence and purpose. Of course, I had read enough about Bosch previously to know that the theological and philosophical meaning of this and most of his other paintings has remained elusive despite numerous attempts to solve their mystery; nevertheless, I could not escape the feeling that in this painting everything fits together and makes sense in some still unknown way.

Since not much is known about Bosch except for the years of his life—ca. 1450–1516, in the town of 's-Hertogenbosch in the Netherlands—speculations have ranged widely about the originality of his art. The sources of his iconography and his ideas have been sought in heretical and doomsday sects, alchemical practices, medieval diableries, astrology, and, most persuasively in my view, in bestiaries, fantastic travel books, and folklore. He has been called a mystic, a moralist, a satirist, a schizophrenic, and even a realist. The Black Plague, the pillage and massacres of the Hundred Years' War, witch burnings, as well as the many of the horrors of our century, came to mind at first seeing the triptych. The extraordinary thing about Bosch is that his vision is somehow both old and modern. I was reminded of Rimbaud's poem "Alchemy of the Verb":

> I accustomed myself to simple hallucinations. I would see quite clearly a mosque in place of a factory, a school of drummers made up of angels, carriages on the roads in the sky, a drawing room at the bottom of a lake; monsters, mysteries; a vaudeville billboard conjured up horrors in my path.

Wherever imagination has reigned supreme in art and literature since Goya and Blake, Bosch suggests himself as a predecessor.

All these and other musings, of course, came to me later. Facing the painting, I was simply trying to orient myself. The temptation of St. Anthony, I recalled, took place in the Egyptian desert, but what I saw before me was a mixture of various kinds of landscapes with buildings from different historical periods.

These ruined towers, tombs, and palaces looked like the stage set of some lost opera co-written by the Marquis de Sade. Temptation of holy men was a standard subject in Bosch's day, but while the tradition counted on a few devils, he made the whole of creation one huge hybrid creature, a demon, as it were, composed of human, animal, vegetable, and inanimate parts.

Exaggeration and distortion of features have always been the staple of comic image making, but Bosch did something else. He was a visionary collagist. He painted as if one could only get at reality by first chopping up everything and then reassembling it again. Like Lautréamont, who wrote in a poem, "beautiful as the encounter of a sewing machine and an umbrella on a dissecting table," he plays the game of joining seemingly unjoinable realities, making the results seem inevitable and leaving us to reconsider the meaning of representation. One of his earliest commentators, Fray Jose de Siguenza, said in 1605, "The difference, which, to my mind, exists between the pictures of this man and those of all others is that the others try to paint man as he appears on the outside, while he alone had the audacity to paint him as he is on the inside." In other words, the Spaniard regarded Bosch's grotesqueries as a form of naturalism.

In the meantime, there is the actual painting to feast one's eyes on. Its sky is thick with odd flying contraptions worthy of a Mad Max movie. Instead of brooms, human beings and devils are riding on fishes, birds, and sailing ships as if this were the most normal thing to do. One demon is doing a handstand on a flying scythe. A stork has a mast of a ship attached to its tail. St. Anthony is saying a prayer on a bullfrog, while next to him an incubus waves a branch with a few dry leaves left on it as if to whip him and make him go faster.

It's much worse down below. A village is on fire, the smoke darkening a portion of the sky. An army, presumably responsible for this, is trotting off merrily, their leader on a white horse. A great solemn allegorical procession of grotesque creatures winds across all three panels. They are dressed as men and women of rank who at first appear to be wearing carnival masks until one notices that their body parts belong to other species. Tree trunks, branches, even an earthen pot and many other unlikely items make up the rest of their bodies. One man wears an owl on his head, another an apple. Inside each being there are multiple monsters hiding, devouring each other or struggling to come out. Cruelty, folly, and lechery reign in every nook and cranny.

What caught my attention right off was the chapel in the central panel, in which Jesus stands with his face turned toward us, apparently distracted from his prayer by the tumult outside. Incredibly, he has been praying to himself crucified on the cross. Next door, there's what looks like a Venetian palazzo. In a tent on its roof a monk and a woman are guzzling wine while over their shoulders a naked woman is diving from the parapet into the canal, and another fat monk, already undressed and with a towel over his shoulders, is cautiously descending the steep steps, watched from inside the palace by a big, old cow and a large bird carrying a tall ladder.

A kind of exhilaration came over me the more I studied the painting. As with the best images in Fellini's and Pasolini's films, or some outrageous comparison in a poem by Russell Edson or James Tate, I was delighted. There's no joy like the one a truly outrageous image on the verge of blasphemy gives. In Bosch, wickedness and innocence are constantly rubbing shoulders. To paint a true picture of the world, he seems to be saying, one needs to include both what people see with eyes open and what they see when they shut their eyes. He does not tell us which is which. For him, the visible and the invisible belong in the same landscape.

It took me a while to begin to pay attention to the saintly hermit and his story. In the left wing we see him helped on his way by three companions, one of whom is Hieronymus himself. St. Anthony is weak from battling the fiends. They're crossing a small bridge, underneath which a monk and a demonic creature are reading—a letter or perhaps a set of instructions about the next round of temptations. A birdlike messenger with a funnel on his head and skates on his feet is delivering a further missive. Over the saint's bowed head, a fish on wheels carts a church steeple. A giant on all fours, right out of *Gulliver's Travels,* with a cloak of grass over his shoulders and an arrow sticking out of his forehead, stares dumbfounded at the goings-on in the sky. Up his rear end, in a small house almost crushed by his weight, there's the entrance to a brothel with a woman peeking out of the window on the lookout for customers.

I was also interested in the fellow with the black stovepipe hat and red robes casually lounging in the central panel with his back to us, who resembles the conjuror in Bosch's famous painting *The Conjuror.* Is he the director of this *Theatrum Mundi?* He calmly observes a pig-headed priest reading from a blue prayer book as if auditioning for a part, while a dead woman with a hollow tree for a bonnet and clutching a living child in her arms waits her turn. Does he himself understand what he has created, or is he as perplexed as we are? Behind his back, a huge tomatolike fruit has cracked open with ripeness. A horse-headed demon strumming a harp leads the way out of it, riding on a plucked goose that wears boots, inside whose severed neck another animal-like face is peeking out.

Each one of us is a synthesis of the real and unreal. We all wear a guise. Even within our own minds, we make constant efforts to conceal ourselves from ourselves, only to be repeatedly found out. Bosch did not need Freud and Jung to tell him that our inner lives are grotesque and scandalous. He also knew something they did fully appreciate. The world inside us is comic. Bosch's paintings cannot be understood without appreciating their riotous humor.

Satan pulled every trick out of his infernal bag, and still the saint went on praying. He saw himself surrounded by a swarm of nightmarish creatures and harems of naked women, and his composure did not leave him. Finally, Satan dispatched the saint's own wife. In the right-wing panel we see her play bawdy peek-a-boo at the entrance to a hollow tree draped over with a red cloth which a drunken demon is drawing back. The saint is as calm as the sunlit meadow at the edge of the woods next to the burning village, or that deer grazing on the roof of the ruin in the central panel. These are the serene corners of life oblivious to tragedy that Auden spoke of in his great poem "Musée des Beaux Arts." Bosch, too, knew that truth. In *The Ascent to Calvary,* painted on the exterior of the right wing of the triptych, we see Christ collapsing under the weight of his cross while a small boy sitting on his father's shoulders is offering an apple to one of the men who has been mistreating our Lord. Again and again Bosch insists that where there is evil, there's also innocence. Nobody ever saw them in such close proximity. That's what makes his paintings so terrifying.

Bosch's initial purpose was probably didactic. Temptation was an occasion to conjure up deadly sins and warn against them, but his imagination subverted the original impulse. I suspect he ended up by enjoying the "demonic beauty" of his creations. Even more subversively, his habit of juxtaposing fantastic with realistic detail gave his paintings a far more ambiguous view of creation and humankind. An art that was supposed to be crystal clear to the faithful ended up being an art rich in unsavory innuendoes. Every artist's imagination holds up a mirror to reality, both the outer and the inner, but how those two realities will finally mingle in the reflection, the owner of the mirror may not even suspect. That is because the devils inside us are all poets, and so, luckily, are the angels.

Out on the street the weather had cleared, so we decided to walk until we found a place to have lunch. Lisbon is a large, bustling city of many hills with breathtaking views of the river Tejo, which flows into the Atlantic a few miles beyond the harbor. What gives the city its distinct character is the maze of old neighborhoods with narrow, cobbled streets, their houses covered with tiles and painted bright colors. A blind man came around the corner and collided with me, giving me a good whack with his white cane. I wish I could say he resembled St. Anthony, but he did not. At the restaurant, a tall, lean, and bearded waiter who served us dried linguica, grilled squid, and chicken and eel stew with shrimp looked vaguely familiar, but we could not place him. We mentioned Vasco da Gama and a few other old navigators, and let it go at that. Late that night, I woke, sat up in bed, and saw the whole painting clearly, and in its central panel the sharp profile of the "conjurer" in red had the pointy beard of our waiter.

The Power of Ambiguity

On Eva Hesse, untitled, ca. 1961, black and brown ink
wash

There are works of art that can be confidently described as
minor and of marginal importance, perhaps even to the artist in
question, that for reasons far from clear, one can't get enough
of. In my own case, I have often been drawn to minimalist works,
from Joseph Cornell to Agnes Martin, where the paucity or the
almost complete absence of narrative, or even of formal com-
plexities, is an invitation to a kind of poetic reverie. I suppose
this is like saying I prefer empty rooms to overdesigned, clut-
tered interiors, spaces where a single chair or an empty birdcage
can do wonders for the imagination. Empty space makes us dis-
cover our inwardness. In such rooms one has the feeling that
time has stopped, that one's solitude and that of the remaining
object are two actors in a metaphysical theater.

This work is one of the series of semiabstract, untitled ink
washes on paper that Eva Hesse composed in 1960 and 1961.
They are like Symbolist poems. Instead of words and images,
smudges, erasures, chance drippings, scribbles, tangled and in-
complete forms, contrasts of shadow and light tease our imagi-
nations. If they had titles, of course, it would be another story.
The title is like a caption to a news photo; it conditions our re-
sponse as it tells us what we are supposed to be seeing. The nam-
ing of the subject matter is already an interpretation. The de-
lightful uncertainty and the free play of associations the untitled
work gives rise to are curtailed for the sake of easy identification.

The ink wash I'm enchanted with appears at first glance less
of a problem. The silhouettes of two tall buildings and perhaps

From *ArtForum* (summer 1999).

even a third one are visible through a small window across a stretch of what very likely could be Central Park in puddles of shadow. It's the brown darkness of an overcast evening with clouds racing and traces of dying light lingering on in the west. There is an air of decrepitude about the scene. Here is the laundry of sundown hung out to dry, as it were, the day's washing, wind-beaten and made grimy by the fumes of the city.

No sooner have I said that than I begin to have my doubts. This window does not really look like a window. It's more like a bamboo picture frame. I have seen such frames on mirrors in people's hallways and in photographs on side tables in a living room where someone once young and handsome is surrounded by exotic knickknacks and memorabilia. How strange to find one enclosing what presumably is an urban scene—unless what we are seeing here is a reflection in a mirror? The point is, it doesn't quite make sense. The frame inside the frame is tilted as if held in someone's unsteady hands. The artist's strategy unsettles our expectations and makes strange what was ordinary only a moment ago.

The more I look at the piece, however, the more I experience its power, the power of its ambiguity. The trap it sets for the imagination is no different from the one found in the sediment on the bottom of a fortuneteller's coffee cup. Blurry outlines, partial views, bizarre cropping elicit a suggestive magic. This drawing is, indeed, like a Symbolist poem. I'm thinking of Mallarmé or Hart Crane at their most hermetic. The secret of that art is not in what you put in, but in how much you leave out. The "poetic" and the "lyrical" states, the Symbolists knew, are beyond exegesis. For instance, when Crane in "To Brooklyn Bridge" describes the lit windows at night as "The city's fiery parcels all undone," the spark of that image transcends any paraphrase. Crane writes: "As a poet I may be possibly more interested in the so-called illogical impingements of the connotations of words on the consciousness (and their combinations and interplay of metaphor on this basis) than I am interested in the preservation of their logically rigid significations at the cost of limiting my subject matter and perception involved in the poem."

Opacities of the evening, a city that appears in ruins, a scene out of a dream, memory of a momentary glance, remains of an old sadness without a cause, the enigma of the real, and the threatening unreality that always hovers over the real. There are times when the world wears the colors and the shadows of our inner life, when reality and imagination appear to be in cahoots. "The imagination is not State: it is the Human Existence itself," Blake wrote. Hesse may think she is drawing a cityscape, while in truth she is dipping into the ink of her own inwardness.

The simplest test for the strength of any work of art is how long one can bear to look at it. This work passes that test for me. I experience in it the shudder of two different selves coming together. I know why Hesse stopped when she did. I picture her pausing with her brush, staring at the drawing, beginning to fall under its spell herself, then for a brief moment fancying someone else seeing what she sees. Being a poet, I know what she was after. I, too, wish to make contact with some unknown person's inner life. Our mutual hope is to bequeath a phrase or an image to the dreamers so that we may live on in their reverie. Because she has done that to me, I have no choice but to revisit this little work, again and again.

Aberlardo Morell's
Poetry of Appearances

Like a slide show of dimly remembered, long unvisited scenes of our lives projected on the wall of a large bedroom languidly criss-crossed by shadows. Half-lit faces and objects made even more strange by their recognizability in the midst of much that remains blurred and fragmented. That uneasy feeling of being uncertain whether I'm dreaming or still lying sleepless. My own room, which I suddenly do not know, its darkness shimmering nebulously as if its walls and ceiling were covered with mirrors. An insomniac's secret collection of grainy black-and-white images that flicker on and off, mystifying in their randomness, in their scrambling of the familiar and the unknown.

We have all awoken in a hotel room or a friend's house after deep sleep not knowing who we are, disoriented about the time and the place, watching the light slip between the drawn curtains to examine a pair of dust balls on the bare floor or woo something we cannot see on the table. Here's the overlooked and invisible dailiness in the process of being unveiled. Framed photograph of the New York skyline no one has looked at closely in ages; sphinxlike armchair; Gideon's Bible perused solely by book lice; unretrieved button, pencil stub, and penny secreted under a dresser or in a shadowy corner; menagerie of water stains caged on the unobserved ceiling. The realm of memory is a hotel-room sewing kit open in my hands. I sit naked in the silence of this unknown room drawing a red thread through the eye of a needle. "It is not seeing—hearing—

From *Face to Face*, the Isabella Gardner Museum's exhibition of Aberlardo Morell's photographs, 1998.

18

feeling," Novalis writes, "it is the combination of all three—more than all three—a sensation of immediate certainty—a view of my truest, most actual (psychic) life." This is what I wish to sew together.

But how? The moment I begin to explain in detail what I have experienced, I run into difficulties. Our strangest dreams, as everybody knows, can never be fully told. Our afternoon daydreams with their play of ephemera are even harder to convey in their elusiveness. As long as we remain quiet, all the nuances of sight and feeling appear in place. It is the very impossibility of describing them that is responsible for the lasting impression they make on us. The world is an apparition at such times; the *unreality* of the real lasts only as long as our silence does.

The same can be said of the experience of viewing a photograph. As long as we only need to point it out to someone without a comment, the way a small child or a weary museum-goer does, and expect merely a nod of agreement in return, innocence reigns. Language fails us as much as it empowers us. What is perceived and what is said rarely match. We approximate, we invent, we seek the help of metaphors and similes to close the gap. That's why poems get revised and the history of philosophy is three thousand years old. When it comes to immediacy of being, the best words can do is to make a pact with a demon of analogy.

"Such is the photograph, it cannot *say* what it lets us see," writes Roland Barthes. Still, the silence of the image invites a dialogue, or rather an attempt at ventriloquism—"to bring into correspondence the obscurity of language and the clarity of things," in Blanchot's phrase. Accordingly, my intention here is to tease the photographs of Abe Morell to speak back to me loudly enough so you can overhear our conversation.

> I turn your picture every which way, but you still find a
> way to look elsewhere and so with a calm and almost
> deliberate intention.
>
> Kafka, *Letter to Felice*

It compels me to look at it again—this is how I would define the peculiarity of a memorable photograph. Something in it has become a trap for my imagination. I'm caught between what I see and that which I cannot see, but suspect may be there. It's as if I had suddenly become even more nearsighted than I actually am. I need to squint and close my eyes and open them again. Even a photograph of a blank wall without any scratches is an invitation to enter a labyrinth and be promptly lost.

Let me give an example.

It occurred to me the other day that the way I look at a photograph and respond to its imagery is tied to my first distinct memory of lingering over a photograph. I was not much older than six or seven. One Sunday, in German-occupied Belgrade, I went to visit my great-aunt, an old retired schoolteacher who lived in an apartment cluttered with furniture and paintings of several generations of dead relatives. To occupy myself, I was provided with a thick photo album, but first, I remember, I had to wash my hands thoroughly, not once but twice, after they failed to pass her inspection. That made me take extreme care with the album and pay close attention to every picture.

There were hundreds of them. Unknown men, women, and children in clothes of another era posing in their backyards and gardens, in front of some monument or an early-model car, or in a few cases laid out in open coffins. Among them, I came upon a sepia photograph that I can still see clearly. It is a of young teacher (my great-aunt) standing in front of the blackboard of what looks like a village classroom, smiling faintly at a boy on the other side of the blackboard who is not much older than I was then, and who is pointing at the sentence written in large, ornate letters, so perfectly legible I have no difficulty reading it even today:

SILENCE IS GOLDEN.

The boy appears ill at ease. His hair is cut so short, his head appears shaven. He wears a suit of a rough cloth that must have made him itch, but with a white shirt open at the neck. It must have been a special occasion, the photographer making a rare visit to a remote village. Three other students with similarly cropped hair are visible in the front seats with their backs to the camera. Although I cannot see their faces, I know their eyes are on the teacher and not on the charts and maps hanging on the wall to the side, which, in any case, are blurred. On that same wall, there's also a window with black panes, giving the false impression that the night had already fallen outdoors.

My great-aunt, who is seen in profile, wears a dark, Sunday kind of dress, and has her hair cut so it just barely covers her ears, causing her long, pale, muscular neck to stand out with determination. I immediately notice her resemblance to my father, who at the moment I'm studying the photograph is missing in the war, and that makes it very spooky.

For years, every time I called on my great-aunt, I asked for the photo album so I could take another long look at the fading photograph. The enigma of "them" still standing there and of myself watching them seemed inexhaustible to me. Here was, in the words of Giorgio de Chirico, "a solemn sheet of paper witnessed by a moment and stamped by eternity." I have forgotten much in my life, but I can still visualize the small white scar on the head of one of the students with his back turned to me. Against all probabilities, this unremarkable scene continues to enrich my oneiric life.

Moments far apart in time come together thanks to photographs. Someone's old reality becomes my new reality. How astonishing that is! After a while, the space of every closely observed photograph becomes an inhabited space. The real and the imaginary take turns exchanging identities. If there's an empty seat in the 1900s classroom, and there happens to be one, I find myself seated in it with my shoulders hunched and my face turned away from the camera, of course. The same is true of many other powerful photographs in whose corners I've been hiding for years.

&

"It is important to see what is invisible to others," Robert Frank maintains, and who could disagree? Morell stares at drops of water until he notices their resemblance to letters of the alphabet. There's an air of clairvoyance about his photographs. He wants the unseen to show itself, the marvelous to happen.

How does Abe Morell go about doing that?

He turns a room, he tells us, into a camera obscura by covering its windows with black plastic so that it is completely dark. Then he makes a three-eighths-inch hole looking out at something interesting. "What happens (next)," he says, "is that through this small opening a fairly sharp, upside-down image of the outdoors appears on the wall opposite the hole." After his eyes accustom themselves to the dark, he gets his view camera and focuses on the projection on the wall. Chance and strict calculation combine to bring the images from outside into the room.

Calculation is present in the way Morell explores the optical properties of the camera, varying, for instance, the size of the pinhole, and chance comes into play during the long exposure of about eight hours, as he's not able to predict how the weather and light will change and what random images may yet drift in from the street. His aim is to surprise himself and to defamiliarize and undermine our habitual way of experiencing our surroundings by introducing a troublemaking ambiguity between illusion and reality. When chance is invited in, when it cooperates as it does here, it opens a door to what is not ordinarily visible. Chance, the redeemer, needs the camera obscura to show us the poetry of appearances that's always around us.

The quest of the ordinary, in Stanley Cavell's phrase, is the great project of modern literature and art. Underwritten by Emerson and Thoreau more than a hundred years ago, the inexhaustible power of common objects continues to be a preoccupation of some of our best photographers and poets today. This may turn out be the most original undertaking of the long twentieth century: the quest for the magic substance to be found in the ordinary. To attempt this it was necessary to peek under our beds and into the darkest corners of our rooms.

"The soul stays home," Emerson told us, and Abe Morell concurs. The philosopher Seneca claimed that he could not philosophize in a palace, but only in a pauper's room where one sleeps and daydreams on a pile of straw. A lived room is a trope factory. Its walls and ceiling have been read like a mystery story. The emptier the room is, the greater the reverie. Think of Morell's images of Manhattan caught through camera obscura in empty rooms. Morell's photographs are spirit catchers. They objectify our inner life.

"Every photograph is in a way a test for the viewer's imagination," writes Mary Price in *A Strange Confined Space,* her invaluable book on photography. This is where the poetry comes in. It is the poet in ourselves who, closing the eyes, enters the imagination's dark room to recover the speech that bridges the gap between image and word. In that sense, photography is a "medium" in its true sense. It is both a technique and an instrument of the spirit.

ð

Morell titles are usually specific and matter of fact: "Paper Bag," "Brady Looking at His Shadow," "Two Forks under Water," "Camera Obscura Image of the Sea in the Attic," "Dictionary," and so on. We are given the actual, what is in front of the camera, and it's up to us to do the rest. The alternative would be furnishing the photographs with the kind of titles the Surrealists used to love to give their paintings and sculptures, titles in which the real is already renamed: "Palace at 4 A.M.," "Chinese Nightingales," "The Snake Charmer," "Immaculate Conception," "Child's Brain," "Enigma of the Day," "Captain Cook's Last Voyage," etc. What we see and what we are told we are seeing are intentionally at odds in such works.

Not so with Morell. First take a good look at what is in fact there, he's telling us with his titles. Admire the formal qualities of this open brown paper bag sitting on the floor or this toy horse. The commonplace object is singled out, brought out of its anonymity, so that it stands before us fully revealed in its uniqueness and its otherness. In the metaphysical solitude of the object we catch a glimpse of our own. Here is the unknowable ground of appearances, that *something* that is always there without being perceived, the world in its nameless, uninterpreted presence which the camera makes visible. That's what casts the spell on me in Morell's photographs: the evidence that our daily lives are the site of momentary insights and beauties which lie around us to be recovered.

The photographer and the poet share a love for unusual images. Both arts are about intuiting resemblances, noticing how a tower of children's blocks can mean more than itself. The ideal is to arrive at an image that will imprint itself on memory and become inexhaustible to the imagination. Who hasn't made towers of blocks, playing cards, or pennies and grown breathless as the tower begins to sway? The trick is to see the tower from underneath, to make ourselves as small as some imaginary pedestrian looking up at its commanding presence. The game being played is the game of becoming smaller or bigger to acquire a new point of view as one yields to the imaginary.

"The individual is not the sum of his common impressions but of his unusual ones," says Gaston Bachelard. Often, of course, the subject matter explains why we remember certain things better than others. A child lying in a pool of blood in the street, or a sheep with two heads at the country fair, is not easily forgotten. But, and this is worth reminding ourselves of, we also remember empty rooms, "certain slants of light," tree shadows on the ceiling, odd stains on the bare wood floor. Memory's museum has room for both the assassinations of presidents and the image of our grandmother's black comb with a few white hairs in it in the back of a rarely opened drawer.

❧

What is astonishing about Morell's photographs is their ability to give this old world a new look. What is this he's got here? we continually ask. Morell has found a way to domesticate the fantastic. It seems perfectly natural to find the reflection of sea waves on the ceiling of an attic. How delightful it must be to stretch out in a bed with the upside-down image of the Empire State Building and midtown Manhattan hovering over one's head! Morell's is a magical-realist show. Nothing is quite what it appears to be. Mirage and reality perform side by side, providing a new aesthetic experience for the viewer.

His photographs of open art books are a part of the same strategy. The camera is held up to the book at a reader's distance, or, more accurately, at a nearsighted reader's distance. Or even better, this could be the solitary child's view, the child who has just begun to imagine stepping into the picture in the book. Who hasn't done that? This is how children always read their stories, as Walter Benjamin reminds us:

Children know such pictures like their own pockets; they have searched through them in the same way and turned them inside out, without forgetting the smallest thread or a piece of cloth. And if in the colored engraving, children's imaginations can fall into reverie, the black-and-white woodcut or the plain prosaic illustration draws them out of themselves.

Who can refuse the temptation to climb into Morell's huge dictionary, whose pages invite us to climb them providing we can make ourselves very tiny? The smaller I can become in my imagination, the more marvelous the world becomes. This coliseum of Piranesi is now as immense for me as the universe. His photographs prove that the whole of creation is a realm of pure imagination. The world is a big, thick book full of wonders admiring themselves through our eyes.

Morell speaks of his new work done in the Gardner Museum as of "marrying faces." "I just love the idea," he says, "that a black janitor can portray the same intensity as a young cocky Rembrandt." We have all had the experience of catching someone viewing a portrait they resemble. The museums in northern Italy are full of madonnas who could have stepped down from the paintings. To discover the same thing in America with its diverse population gives one the feeling of Whitman's democratic vistas. "You shall stand by my side and look in the mirror with me," the old poet said, and he meant all of us. As Morell says: "To my mind I think that guards end up looking at these works of art longer than any scholar and that some of the people who work here are as beautiful and haunting as anything on the wall."

In the same letter to me, Morell speaks about wanting to "combine things like a close-up of a beautiful silver tea set on display with a secretary's coffee mug next to her computer." This, I think, is the heart of his vision—the perception of similarity in disparate things, the bringing of two separate realities together, not to cancel out their individual properties, but to perform an alchemical wedding. A visual innovation is the result of collaging, of discovering the figurative in the literal. To find resemblance, for Morell, is to find an image of something never seen before, and that's no small accomplishment for any photographer or any poet.

Verbal Image

An image made up entirely of words? That may sound like a magician's sleight of hand, and in many ways it is one, except that even its cleverest practitioners do not know all its secrets. For instance, how many words are necessary to do the trick? It doesn't have to be many, but when they do their work, something or someone we have never met before suddenly materializes before us.

"His wife looks like a stork," we overhear someone say on the street, and we instantly start furnishing the rest. She is tall, thin-legged, wears short skirts, and keeps her head hanging low. And that's just the beginning. Once our imagination gets cued up, it fills the blanks. Both good writers and good gossips know that all one needs to do is plant a hint. Isaac Babel describes someone—I forget who—as having "a soul as gentle and pitiless as the soul of a cat," and the face of a chubby little boy who likes to pluck the legs off flies pops into my head.

It's much harder if I'm the one who is trying to make a verbal image. I wish to nail with a quick phrase or two someone's idiosyncrasy. I know that lengthy description of their physical appearance or quips about their psychological traits won't catch it. What I'm looking for is that fleeting moment when an expression on their face, a gesture, a look in their eyes divulges something of their true character.

I remember my mother sitting one late October afternoon in the garden of a nursing home with a red shawl over her shoulders and a small book in her lap. I had come to pay her a visit, was told where she was, and stood by her side unobserved. It was

From *Reflections in the Glass Eye: Works from the International Center of Photography Collection* (New York: Little Brown, 1999).

very quiet. Once in a long while she looked up with the day's fading sunlight on her face as if to ponder some serious matter she had just read and reread. The sky was clear and open to view because the leaves had already fallen and lay still around her thick-soled, black shoes. I wrote a poem about it, but had no confidence that my work conveyed what I saw and felt. It was discernible to me, but perhaps obscure to the reader. The alchemy of turning what is visible to us into what is visible to others is what all the arts are about.

Despite the heavy odds, it can be done. "He was a white man with greased black hair and a greased black look to his suit. He moved like a crow"; this is how Flannery O'Connor describes a steward seating people in the dining car of a train. She writes elsewhere of "a young woman in slacks, whose face was as broad and as innocent as a cabbage and was tied around with a green hand-kerchief that had two points on the top like rabbit's ears." Our identities are secretive; they like to hide in plain view. The art of portraiture and the art of caricature are near cousins. Both zero in on some overlooked detail invisible until that very moment. A verbal image is the equivalent of a snapshot, except in this case the reader supplies the flash.

Buster Keaton

Only recently, with their issue on videotape, have all the films of Buster Keaton become widely available. It's likely one may have seen "The General" (1926) in some college course, or caught a couple of shorts at some museum retrospective of silent comedy, but such opportunities were rare and for most moviegoers in this country nonexistent. When Keaton's name came up, people who knew who he was would often say how much they preferred his laid-back stoicism to Chaplin's sentimentality, admitting in the same breath that, regretfully, they had not seen one of his films in a long time.

I first heard about Buster Keaton from my grandmother, who was also of the opinion that he was the funniest of the silent-movie comedians. This didn't make much sense to me at the time since she described him as a man who never smiled, who always stayed dead serious while she and the rest of the audience screamed with delight. I remember trying to imagine his looks from what she told me, going so far as to stand in front of a mirror with a deadpan expression until I could bear it no longer and would burst out laughing. In the early post–World War II days in Belgrade, there was still a movie theater showing silent films. My grandmother took me to see Chaplin, Harold Lloyd, the cross-eyed Ben Turpin, but for some reason we never saw Keaton. Is that him? I would occasionally nudge her and whisper when some unfamiliar, somber face appeared on the screen. Weary of my interruptions, which disrupted her passionate absorption in films, one day upon returning home she produced a pile of old illustrated magazines. She made for herself her customary cup of

From *Writers at the Movies,* ed. Jim Shepard (New York: HarperCollins, 2000).

chamomile tea and started thumbing through the dusty issues, allowing me to do the same after she was through. I remember a black-and-white photograph of a sea of top hats at some king's or queen's funeral; another of a man lying in a pool of blood in the street; and the face of a beautiful woman in a low-cut party dress watching me intently from a table in an elegant restaurant, her breasts partly exposed. My grandmother never found Keaton. It took me another seven years to actually see a film of his. By the time I did, my grandmother was dead, the year was 1953, and I was living in Paris.

Most probably, I was playing hooky that afternoon, sneaking into a cinema when I should've been in class, but there was Buster Keaton finally on the screen, wearing a porkpie hat and standing on the sidewalk at the end of a long breadline. The line keeps moving, but for some reason the two fellows standing in front of him do not budge. They are clothing-store dummies, but Buster does not realize that. He takes a pin out of his lapel and pricks one of the slowpokes, but there is no reaction; meanwhile the line up ahead grows smaller and smaller as each man is handed a loaf of bread. Then Buster has an idea. He pricks himself to see if the pin works. At that moment the store owner comes out, sticks his hand out to check for rain, and takes the two fully dressed dummies under his arms and carries them inside.

A few other gags have remained vivid in my memory from that first viewing of Keaton's shorts. In the one called "Cops" (1922), Buster buys an old horse and a wagon. The horse is deaf and doesn't hear his commands, so he puts a headset over the horse's ears, sits in the driver's seat, and tries to telephone the horse. In another scene, he pats the same horse on the head, and the horse's false teeth fall out. In the short called "The Playhouse" (1921), Keaton plays all the roles. He's the customer buying the ticket, the conductor of the orchestra and all his musicians, the nine tap dancers, the stagehands, and everyone in the audience, both the grown-ups and the children.

As for the appearance of Buster himself, everything about him was at odds. He was both strange looking and perfectly ordinary. His expression never changed, but his eyes were eloquent, intelligent and sad at the same time. He was of small stature, compact and capable of sudden astonishing acrobatic feats. Keaton, who was born in 1895 in a theatrical boarding-house in Piqua, Kansas, started in vaudeville when he was three years old. His father, the son of a miller in Oklahoma, had left his parents to join a medicine show. That's where he met his future wife. Her father was coproprietor of one such show. For the next twenty years, they toured nationally, often in the company of famous performers of the day, such as Harry Houdini. Eventually, the Three Keatons, as they were called, developed a vaudeville comic act that consisted of acrobatic horseplay centered on the idea of a hyper child and his distraught parents. Buster hurled things at his Pop, swatted him with fly swatters and brooms while his father swung him around the stage by means of a suitcase handle strapped to the boy's back. What looked like an improvised roughhouse was really a carefully planned series of stunts. The point is worth emphasizing since it was with such and similar acts in vaudeville that silent-film comedy stagecraft originated.

The first principle of Keaton's comic personae is endless curiosity. Reality is a complicated machine running in mysterious ways whose working he's trying to understand. If he doesn't crack a smile, it's because he is too preoccupied. He is full of indecision, and yet he appears full of purpose. "A comic Sisyphus," Daniel Mowes called him. "OUR HERO CAME FROM *NOWHERE*," a caption in "High Sign" (1920) says, continuing: "HE WASN'T GOING *ANYWHERE* AND GOT KICKED OFF *SOMEWHERE*." Bedeviled by endless obstacles, Buster is your average slow-thinking fellow, seeking a hidden logic in an illogical world. "Making a funny picture," he himself said, "is like assembling a watch; you have to be 'sober' to make it tick."

In the meantime, my mother, brother, and I were on the move again. We left Paris for New York. A few years later I was back in France as an American soldier. It turned out that they were still showing Keaton films in small cinemas on the Left Bank. That's when I saw most of the shorts and a few of the full-length films like "The General" and "The Navigator" (1924). Since there always seemed to be a Keaton festival in Paris, a day came when I took my children to see the films. They loved them and made me see the gags with new eyes since they often noticed comic subtleties I had missed.

"A good comedy can be written on a postcard," Keaton said. A comic story told silently, that even a child could enjoy, we should add. Is it the silence of the image that frees the comic imagination? Of course. Think of cartoons. In silent films we can't hear the waves, the wind in the leaves, the cars screeching to a halt, the guns going off, so we fill in the sound. For instance, in Keaton's full-length film "Seven Chances" (1926), a man learns that his grandfather is leaving him seven million dollars providing he is married before seven o'clock in the evening on his twenty-seventh birthday, which just happens to be that day. He proposes to every woman he knows and is rebuffed, and places an ad in the afternoon paper, explaining his predicament and promising to be in church at five that afternoon. Several hundred prospective brides, old and young, show up wearing bridal gowns, one of them even arriving on roller skates. The prospective bridegroom runs for his life, and the brides stampede after him through busy downtown Los Angeles. All of us who saw the movie can still hear the sound of their feet.

In an essay entitled "How to Tell a Story," Mark Twain makes the following observations:

> To string incongruities and absurdities together in a wandering and sometime purposeless way, and seem innocently unaware that they are absurdities, is the basis of American art. Another feature is the slurring of the point. A third is the dropping of a studied remark apparently without knowing it, as if one were thinking aloud. The fourth and the last is the pause.

Twain explains what he means:

> The pause is an exceedingly important feature in any kind of story, and a frequently recurring feature, too. It is a dainty thing, a delicate, and also uncertain and treacherous; for it must be exactly the right length—no more and no less—or it fails of its purpose and makes trouble. If the pause is too short, the important point is passed and the audience have had the time to divine that a surprise is intended—and then you can't surprise them, of course.

Comedy is about timing, faultless timing. It's not so much what the story is about, but the way it is told, with its twists and surprises, that makes it humorous. Keaton draws a hook with chalk on the wall and hangs his coat on it. A brat in the theater drops his half-sucked lollipop from the balcony on an elegant lady in a box who picks it up and uses it as a lorgnette. The hangman uses a blindfold intended for the victim to polish the medal on his jacket. The shorts, especially, are full of such wild inventions. No other silent-film comic star was as ingenious.

Among hundreds of examples from Keaton's films, one of my favorites comes from the short "Cops." At the annual New York City policemen's parade, Buster and his horse and wagon find themselves in the midst of the marching cops. Buster wants to light a cigarette, and is searching his pockets for matches, when a bomb thrown by an anarchist from a rooftop lands next to him on the seat with its short fuse already sizzling. There's a pause, "an inspiring pause," as Twain says, building itself to a deep hush. When it has reached its proper duration, Buster picks up the bomb absentmindedly, lights his cigarette with it as if this were the most normal thing to do, and throws it back over his head.

The short "Cops" is paradigmatic Keaton. Again, the plot is simplicity itself. In the opening scene we see Buster behind bars. The bars turn out to belong to the garden gate of the house of a girl he is in love with. "I won't marry you till you become a businessman," she tells him. Off he goes, through a series of adventures, first with a fat police detective in a rush to grab a taxi, the contents of whose wallet end up in Buster's hands. Next, he is conned by a stranger who sells him a load of furniture on the sidewalk, pretending he is a starving man being evicted. The actual owner of the furniture and his family are simply moving to another location. When Buster starts to load the goods into the wagon he has just bought, the owner mistakes him for the moving man they've been expecting. His trip across town through the busy traffic culminates when he finds himself at the head of the police parade passing the flag-draped reviewing stand where the chief of police, the mayor, and the young woman he met at the garden gate are watching in astonishment. Still, the crowd is cheering, and he thinks it's for him. After he tosses the anarchist's bomb and it explodes, all hell breaks loose. "GET SOME COPS TO PROTECT OUR POLICE-MEN," the mayor orders the chief of police. People run for cover, the streets empty, the entire police force takes after the diminutive hero.

What an irony! Starting with love and his desire to better himself and impress the girl he adores, all he gets in return is endless trouble. It's the comic asymmetry between his extravagant hope and the outcome that makes the plot here. The early part of the movie, with its quick shuffle of gags, gives the misleading impression of a series of small triumphs over unfavorable circumstances. Just when Buster thinks he has his bad luck finally conquered, disaster strikes again. The full force of law and order, as it were, descends on his head. Innocent as he is, he is being pursued by hundreds of policemen. Whatever he attempts to do, all his stunts and clever evasions, come to nothing because he cannot outrun his destiny. After a long chase, he ends up, unwittingly, at the very door of a police precinct. The cops are converging on him from all sides like angry hornets, blurring the entrance in their frenzy to lay their nightsticks on him, but incredibly Buster crawls between the legs of the last cop, he himself now dressed in a policeman's uniform. Suddenly alone on the street, he pulls a key out of his pocket, locks the precinct's door from the outside, and throws the key into a nearby trashcan. At that moment, the girl he is smitten with struts by. He looks soulfully at her, but she lifts her nose even higher and walks on. Buster hesitates for a moment, then goes to the trashcan and retrieves the key. "No guise can protect him now that his heart has been trampled on," Gabriella Oldham says in her magnificent study of Keaton's shorts. At the end of the film, we see him unlocking the door and being pulled by hundreds of policemen's hands into the darkness of the building.

What makes Keaton unforgettable is the composure and dignity he maintains in the face of what amounts to a deluge of misfortune in this and his other films. It's more than anyone can bear, we think. Still, since it's the American Dream Buster is pursuing, we anticipate a happy ending, or at least the hero having the last laugh. That's rarely the case. Keaton's films, despite their laughs, have a melancholy air. When a lone tombstone with Buster's porkpie hat resting on it accompanies THE END in "Cops," we are disconcerted. The images of him running down the wide, empty avenue, of his feeble attempt to disguise himself by holding his clip-on tie under his nose to simulate a mustache and goatee, are equally poignant. Let's see if we can make our fate laugh, is his hope. Comedy at such a high level says more about the predicament of the ordinary individual in the world than tragedy does. If you seek true seriousness and you suspect that it is inseparable from laughter, then Buster Keaton ought to be your favorite philosopher.

Poetry and History

I have in mind the history of murder. Massacre of the innocent is a nearly universal historical experience, and perhaps never more so than in the last hundred years. Deranged leaders with huge armies and brutal secret police out to kill, gas, and imprison every one of us for the sake of some version of a glorious future, while being idealized and cheered by their followers, is what we have had to live through. "It takes a great ideal to produce a great crime," the historian Martin Malia writes. The problem for those constructing heaven on earth is that there is always an individual, a class of people, or a national, ethnic, or religious group standing in the way. Communism alone killed between 80 and 100 million people. It is also worth remembering the millions of displaced people, all those made destitute for life as a result of these ideological bloodbaths. Is poetry a holiday from such realities? It certainly can be. There are many examples of poets who, judging by their work, never read a newspaper in their lives. Still, a poet who consistently ignores the evils and injustices that are part of his or her own times is living in a fool's paradise.

History written by historians, as we know, speculates about the causes and meanings of cataclysmic events and the motives of the statesmen involved in them. Foucault says: "We want historians to confirm our belief that the present rests upon profound intentions and immutable necessities. But the true historical sense confirms our existence among countless lost events without a landmark or a point of reference." This is where the poets come in. In place of the historian's broad sweep, the poet

A version of this essay appeared in *The Uncertain Certainty* (Ann Arbor: University of Michigan Press, 1986).

gives us a kind of reverse history of what in the great scheme of things are often regarded as "unimportant" events, the image of a dead cat, say, lying in the rubble of a bombed city, rather than the rationale for that air campaign. Poetry succeeds at times in conveying the pain of individuals caught in the wheels of history. One of the most terrifying lines of twentieth-century poetry is by the Italian poet Salvatore Quasimodo, who speaks of "the black howl of the mother gone to meet her son crucified on a telephone pole." The individual who is paying for the intellectual vanity, fascination with power, and love of violence of some monster on the world's stage is the one that I care about. Perhaps only in lyric poetry can that mother's howl be heard as loudly as it ought to be.

Nearly everyone who made history in the last century believed that the mass killing of the innocent was permissible. This is true not only of the Nazis and the Communists, whose savageries were perpetrated in the name of an idea, but also of the democratic countries that in their many bombing campaigns, unintentionally and often intentionally, slaughtered hundreds of thousands. We Americans often fought evil with evil, and while we did so, many innocents caught in-between paid the price. No matter what politicians and military men tell us, bombing has always been a form of collective punishment. Theoreticians of air power from Giulio Douhet to Curtis LeMay have never concealed that purpose. They argue that in war there must not be any differentiation between military personnel and civilians. With the help of new technologies, total war and mass terror became a reality for many human beings in the last hundred years. Bombs falling from the sky, armies slaughtering each other, civilians fleeing for their lives, the orphan factories working around the clock—that's what the poet has to think about or ignore.

In the days of mounted cavalries, foot soldiers, and cannons dragged by horses, the civilian population had to worry about a long siege, eventual conquest with accompanying pillage and rape, and an occasional burning of a city, but those things were not in themselves primary objects of military action. The first bombs were dropped in the mid–nineteenth century from balloons, dirigibles, and other such lighter-than-air vessels. Actually, it was in the war of 1849 that Austrians attempted to drop thirty-pound bombs on Venice using paper balloons. In the absence of photos, one imagines a bird's-eye postcard view of the city with its canals, boats, churches, palazzos, and piazzas. The sky is blue, the gulls are flying, and the streets are teeming with humanity as if it were carnival time. A red and white balloon drifts dreamily over the highest steeples, is about to drop its single explosive device, when an unexpected gust of wind sweeps it out of range and far off into the blue Adriatic. Nowadays, whether conventional or nuclear bombs are being utilized, everyone expects to be a sitting duck. Mass terror on a scale impossible to imagine in previous centuries is a real possibility, an option carefully studied by every military power in the world.

If not for the invention of photography and eventually television, our image of war would still come from paintings of historical scenes and illustrations for daily newspapers. Even the burning villages and firing squads in such illustrations, if you have ever seen them, have an idyllic air about them. We end up being more interested in the artist's skill in rendering the event than in the horror of what is taking place. Unhappily for warmongers everywhere, however, the fate of soldiers and civilians in wartime has been amply documented. To thumb through a book of old news photos of battlefield carnage, or watch documentary footage of an air raid on Berlin in progress, is a deeply sobering experience. Here's a row of burnt and still smoldering buildings of which only the outside walls remain. Rubble lies in the streets. The sky is black except for dragons of flames and swirling smoke. Most probably there are people buried under the rubble. We can't hear their voices, but we know for certain that they are there. I remember a photo of a small girl running toward a camera in a bombed city somewhere in China. No one else is in sight. There are thousands of such haunting images from the many wars fought in the last century. After almost a hundred years of bombing, it takes a staggering insensitivity and insouciance not to acknowledge what a bombing raid does in an urban area and who its true victims are.

Given the shocking number of casualties in bombings of cities, there are good reasons no one wishes to dwell on them much, except someone like me who had the unenviable luck of being bombed by both the Nazis and the Allies. Here are some appalling figures: 40,000 dead in the Blitz; another 40,000 dead in Hamburg in 1943; 100,000 in Dresden in 1945; 100,000 in Tokyo in 1945, plus Hiroshima and Nagasaki, where another 135,000 perished. And the list goes on. There's Berlin, and many other German and Japanese cities, and more recently Hanoi, where an estimated 65,000 died, and finally Baghdad. As John Kenneth Galbraith pointed out in an article in the *New York Times,* the ordinary citizens of Germany, Japan, Korea, Vietnam, and Iraq were far more in fear of our bombers than of their own oppressive governments, and why wouldn't they be? In Germany alone, 593,000 German civilians were killed and over 3.3 million homes destroyed. In Japan, without counting the victims of the atomic bombs, over 300,000 people perished just in 1945. Are deaths of enemy noncombatants truly of so little consequence? The answer—judging by the long, cruel history of the twentieth century's bombings—is a resounding yes. It is also worth remembering that the bombing of civilians is rarely punished as a crime. These air campaigns are based on the ridiculous premise that the dictator cares about the welfare of his own people and will not permit the destruction of his country to continue. Of course, if he really did give a damn he would not be a dictator. What happens, instead, is that the two warring sides become allies against the civilians in the middle. This may sound like an outrageous assertion to someone who has never had bombs drop on his or her head from a few thousand feet, but I speak from experience. That's exactly how it feels on the ground. In modern warfare, it has become much safer to be in the military than to be a noncombatant.

Of course, there's nothing reliable about any one of these rounded-off figures of casualties. Bombing history plays games with numbers to conceal the fate of individuals. The deaths of women and children are an embarrassment. All religious and secular theories of "just war," from St. Augustine to the United Nations charter, caution against their indiscriminate slaughter. Consequently, the numbers vary widely, depending on the source and the agenda of the historian, when they are not entirely omitted from history books. Even when they do appear, they are as incomprehensible as astronomical distances or the speed of light. A figure like 100,000 conveys horror on an abstract level. It is a rough estimate since no one really knows for sure. It is easily forgotten, easily altered. A number like 100,001, on the other hand, would be far more alarming. That lone, additional individual would restore the reality to the thousands of casualties. When one adds to these figures the sum total of people who were bombed and somehow survived, the numbers become truly unimaginable.

My own story belongs with those of these anonymous multitudes. Here's a little poem based on a few images of the bombing of Belgrade in 1941 from a World War II documentary.

Cameo Appearances

I had a small, nonspeaking part
In a bloody epic. I was one of the
Bombed and fleeing humanity.
In the distance the great leader
Crowed like a rooster from a balcony,
Or was it a great actor
Impersonating the great leader.

That's me, I said to the kiddies.
I'm squeezed between the man
With two bandaged hands raised
And the old woman with her mouth open
As if she were showing us a tooth

That hurts badly. The hundred times
I rewound the tape, not once
Could they catch sight of me
In that huge gray crowd,
That was like any other gray crowd.

Trot off to bed, I said finally.
I know I was there. One take
Is all they had time for.
We ran and the planes grazed our hair,
And then they were no more
As we stood dazed in the burning city,
But, of course, they didn't film that.

The beauties of Nature, the mysteries of the Supreme Being, and the torments of love are still with us, but a shadow lies over them. "God is afraid of man . . . man is a monster, and history has proved it," says Cioran. Some of us are who we are because of that kind of thinking. For example, I remember a night during the Vietnam War. I had returned home late after a swell evening on the town and happened to turn on a TV channel where they were presenting a summary of that day's action on the battlefield. I was already undressed and sipping a beer when they showed a helicopter strafing some small running figures who were supposedly Vietcong and were more likely just poor peasants caught in the cross fire. I could see the bodies twitch and jump as they were hit by a swarm of bullets. It occurred to me that this had been filmed only hours ago and here I was in my bedroom, tired but no longer sleepy, feeling the monstrosity of watching someone's horror from the comfort of my bedroom as if it were a spectator sport.

Can one be indifferent to the fate of the blameless and go about as if it doesn't matter? Yes, there have been more than a few fine poets in the history of poetry who had no ethical feelings or interest in other people's sufferings. There is always religion available, of course, or some theory of realpolitik to explain away the awful reality and ease one's conscience. What if one doesn't buy any of these theories—as I do not? Well, then one just writes poems as someone who sees and feels deeply, but who even after a lifetime does not understand the world.

On the Night Train: On Mark Strand

It's a great stroke of luck, when it comes to poetry, that human beings do not know themselves very well. We meet the familiar stranger in our mirror, pretending most days that there's nothing odd about him, nothing worth thinking about, but in fact we know better. "Why am I me? Why not a goldfish in a fish tank in a restaurant somewhere on the outskirts of Des Moines?" Mark Strand asks in The Weather of Words (2000), his fine collection of essays and comic pieces. Poets, like everyone else, do not have the answer. However, here's where the fun starts. In poetry, life's ambiguities are worth more than what can be explained. They cause poems to be written. The true poet, one might say, gropes in the dark. Far from being omniscient on the subject of his work, he is merely a faithful servant of his hunches. The poem, with all its false starts and endless revisions, still mostly writes itself.

There is a good reason for that. The awful truth is that no memorable figure of speech can be willed into existence. They just pop into the poet's head. Consequently no poet can possibly envision the full meaning and the eventual fate of one of his metaphors. For all he knows, it may be in the process of selling his soul to the Devil. The more original the poet, the wider the gap between his intentions and his inventions. Even when they are widely read, much liked, or even belittled, the true nature of many poets' work remains elusive for a long time.

This is certainly the case with Mark Strand. At various times over the last thirty years, he has been regarded as both a Neo-

Review of *The Weather of Words* (2000), *Blizzard of One* (1998), and *Chicken, Shadow, Moon and More* (2000), by Mark Strand. From the *New York Review of Books*, August 10, 2000.

Surrealist and a poet working in the long spent tradition of Modernism. What makes Strand so "uncontemporary" is his conviction that all of poetry, going back to the Greek and Roman poets, is still relevant for someone writing today in Brooklyn or Kansas. In his new book of essays he explains: "I believe that all poetry is formal in that it exists within limits, limits that are either inherited by tradition or limits that language itself imposes. These limits exist in turn within the limits of the individual poet's conception of what is or is not a poem." Poetry's self-reflective nature is his major theme. Whoever reads him in the future will find little of contemporary America in his work. His poems are introspective, obsessively so. If there are tragic and comic moments in them, and there are plenty, they concern solitary, anonymous characters and take place in settings equally nameless. Even though he is looked upon as an established figure, one who was recently named poet laureate of the United States, Strand has been a loner, someone whose best poems, despite his honors, are out of sync with his times.

Since Whitman, most American poets have exerted themselves not to sound too literary. In their efforts to disarm their readers, they take their cue from Emerson's idea of the poet as the representative man. "We are no better than you are," Whitman writes in the 1855 introduction to *Leaves of Grass*. This is not what Strand is after. He is unabashedly elitist and literary. The reader he seeks is a member of a minority, an ideal reader, a total unknown, someone who may not even be born yet. A book of Strand's is like a long night train with a single passenger riding in it. He is bent over with a small flashlight reading from the book of his life. From time to time, he raises his head, straining to glimpse something of the landscape rushing by beyond the dark window, only to catch sight of his ghostly reflection in the glass. He whispers to himself, hoping that he is being overheard.

> In a field
> I am the absence
> of field.
> This is
> always the case.
> Wherever I am
> I am what is missing.

When I walk
I part the air
and always
the air moves in
to fill the spaces
where my body's been.

We all have reasons
for moving.
I move
to keep things whole.
("Keeping Things Whole")

Mark Strand was born in Summerside, Prince Edward Island, Canada, in 1934, of American parents. His father was an executive for Pepsi-Cola and traveled widely, taking his family with him. They lived in Halifax, Montreal, New York, and Philadelphia, as well as in Peru, Columbia, and Mexico. After graduating from Antioch College, Strand studied painting at Yale with Josef Albers. Following the years 1960 and 1961, which he spent on a Fulbright Scholarship in Italy, he enrolled in the Iowa Writers' Workshop and after graduation taught there till 1965. Since that time he has lived in Brazil, Ireland, Italy, New York, New Haven, Charlottesville, Cambridge, Salt Lake City, Baltimore, and Chicago, teaching literature and creative writing. Among American poets, only Elizabeth Bishop may have lived in more places than Strand has, and yet he's rarely a poet of travel. Like Marco Polo in Italo Calvino's *Invisible Cities,* who sought something of his native Venice in every fabulous city he visited as he journeyed across Asia, Strand bumps into himself everywhere. He is a poet, as it were, who is always seated at home in his bathrobe and slippers while being usually in transit.

I first met Strand in New York City at the reading organized by Paul Carroll in 1967 to promote his anthology *Young American Poets.* A tall, handsome, and extremely elegant man, he did not look like a poet. On the other hand, most poets don't look like poets. One is more liable to encounter the type among morticians and flower-shop attendants. Although we imagined our poems to be unmistakably different, the poet James Wright, who introduced us, had our poetry confused. He praised to the skies

43

a poem of mine, calling it Strand's, and vice versa. We, of course, were so honored to have a distinguished older poet speak so well of us we did not dare correct him afterward.

Strand and I belong to a generation of American poets who discovered and were influenced by both European and South American poetry. The 1960s were a great period of translation. Strand himself has translated from both Spanish and Portuguese. Poets like Pablo Neruda, César Vallejo, Vasko Popa, Henri Michaux, Paul Celan, Carlos Drummond de Andrade, Rafael Alberti, Rainer Maria Rilke, Fernando Pessoa, Zbigniew Herbert, Vincent Huidobro, and Robert Desnos, among many others, were closely read and imitated. Our literary historians and critics, who have at best only a superficial knowledge of foreign literatures, habitually overlook these important influences when they write about this period. The issue for poets of any age is how to rejuvenate the lyric poem, and here were various possibilities not to be found in the American poetry of the times. What we admired above all about these foreign poets was the extravagance of their similes and metaphors, the way they let their imaginations run wild. "He is a cosmetician of the ordinary," Strand says of Pablo Neruda in a piece from his new book of essays. Here is the beginning of the Chilean poet's "Death Alone," translated by Angel Flores:

> There are lonely cemeteries,
> graves full of bones without sound,
> the heart passing through a tunnel,
> dark, dark, dark,
> as in a shipwreck we die from within
> as we drown in the heart,
> as we fall out of the skin into the soul.
>
> There are corpses,
> there are feet of cold, sticky clay,
> there is death within bones,
> like pure sound,
> like barking without dogs,
> emanating from several bells, from several graves,
> swelling in the humidity like tears or rain.
> I see, alone, at times
> coffins with sails,

bearing away pallid dead, women with dead tresses,
bakers white as angels,
pensive girls married to public notaries,
coffins ascending the vertical river of the dead,
the purple river,
upstream, with sails filled with the sound of death,
filled by the silent sound of death.

While other American poets were content to make poems by
piling up one image after another in the manner of Neruda,
Strand did something else in his first book, *Reasons for Moving*
(1968). He would take a single image and make a narrative out
of it, the way our dreams do. A mood dredges up an image in a
dream; that image then tells its story. So it is with Strand. Many
of the poems in the book are like dreams, the kinds that leave
us absolutely baffled. A man climbs into a tree and won't come
down. Another fellow stands in front of someone's house for
days on end watching the people inside. A ghost ship floats
through crowded streets. In a town library someone sits eating
poetry. Like the unknown movie projectionist in charge of our
nightly film festival, what Strand finds tantalizing about such
oneiric images is not their psychological content but their po-
etry. The following perceptive comment on Edward Hopper
from Strand's book on the painter is an equally good descrip-
tion of the ambience of many of his poems.

So much of what occurs within a Hopper seems related to
something in the invisible realm beyond its borders: figures
lean toward an absent sun, roads and tracks continue toward
a vanishing point that can only be supposed. Yet Hopper
often establishes the unreachable within his paintings.

In *Stairway*, a small, eerie picture, we look down some
stairs through an open door to a dark, impenetrable massing
of trees or hills directly outside. Everything in the house says,
Go. Everything outside says, Where? All that painting's geom-
etry primes us for is darkly denied us. The open door is not
the innocent passage connecting inside and outside but a ges-
ture paradoxically designed to keep us where we are.

In his next book of poems, *Darker* (1970), some of Strand's
American influences became apparent. Wallace Stevens and

Elizabeth Bishop at their most surrealist and obscure are both present. Strand writes: "In Stevens, argument tends to be discontinuous, hidden, mysterious, or simply not there. More often, what we experience is the power of the word or the phrase to enchant." These are his strategies too. What he is aiming at, in book after book, is a short lyric poem perfectly executed:

> When I say "lyric poems," I mean poems that manifest musical properties, but are intended to be read or spoken, not sung. They are usually brief, rarely exceeding a page or two, and have about them a degree of emotional intensity, or an urgency that would account for their having been written at all. At their best, they represent the shadowy, often ephemeral motions of thought and feeling, and do so in ways that are clear and comprehensible. Not only do they fix in language what is often most elusive about our experience, but they convince us of its importance, even its truth. Of all literary genres, the lyric is the least changeable. Its themes are rooted in the continuity of human subjectivity and from antiquity have assumed a connection between privacy and universality.

A poem that invites the reader to endless reverie is Strand's ideal. *Darker* is a young man's book, which atypically is obsessed with death. As he aptly points out, the business of dying is the central concern of lyric poetry. The early deaths of his mother and father and the accompanying feeling of irretrievable loss haunt him. The heart of the lyric for Strand is the place "where elegy imagines a future that mourns the past." The heightened sense of the self that accompanies such knowledge is his subject. "The poem celebrates the sad moment when we become history," he observes in an essay on a poem by Charles Wright, but this pathos is equally true of his poems. Strand is an inward exile. His poems make me think of immigrants' suitcases full of old family photographs; they take them out from time to time, and look at them until they find some small detail, never noticed before, that breaks their hearts. Strangely, and this may be its whole point, nostalgia for the past is really a covert way of making the present more poignant, more real.

The Prediction

That night the moon drifted over the pond,
turning the water to milk, and under
the boughs of the trees, the blue trees,
a young woman walked and for an instant

the future came to her:
rain falling on her husband's grave, rain falling
on the lawns of her children, her own mouth
filling with cold air, strangers moving into her house,

a man in her room writing a poem, the moon drifting into it,
a woman strolling under its trees, thinking of death,
thinking of him thinking of her, and the wind rising
and taking the moon and leaving the paper dark.

Another peculiarity of Strand's poem is the way he slows down
the clock. No sooner has the poem begun than weariness takes
over; everything winds down as if one were watching an Anto-
nioni movie. For Strand, in an infinite universe, a beginning is as
meaningless as is the end. What they both mask is a deep un-
derlying stillness at the core of things. A continuous present in
which nothing happens, but which is rich in omens and intu-
itions, is his idea of paradise. Does this make Strand a mystic?
Yes, but a very peculiar one. What interests him about the mo-
ment is not its metaphysics but its aesthetics. His hope is to con-
vey the beauty that accompanies such sublime experiences.

He can't be serious, you are probably saying to yourself. Who
still believes in beauty with a capital B? Well, some poets do.
Poets believe in many such unfashionable sentiments that most
of today's literary and art critics would find laughable. Be that
as it may, there's a serious question lurking in Strand's poetry:
Is it the truth or is it the beauty of some philosophical or reli-
gious system that we are attracted to? Are we simply pulling wool
over our eyes when we insist that it is the truth? What if it's the
elegance of the argument that makes it convincing? Strand, I
would say, is pretty sure that the supreme philosophical prob-
lem is one of aesthetics. He trusts in good taste more than he
does in abstract ideas.

His next book, *The Story of Our Lives* (1973), is very different.

Strand had been reading Wordsworth's *The Prelude,* and the au-
tobiographical element in these poems is even more overt.
Some of them are quite long, and nearly all are narrative, but in
an odd, circular way. They replay a single fragment of memory
over and over again. Strand is like someone in a police lab en-
larging a photograph to identify a face or an important detail.
If only I could insert myself back into that lost moment, he
thinks, I could begin once more the story of my life as if it had
not been written yet. "Untelling," "Elegy for My Father," "In Cel-
ebration," "The Room," and the book's title poem are some of
the most moving poems Strand has written.

In *Late Hour* (1976), he returned to shorter poems, some
more open in form, but thematically his range remained no-
tably small. "My Mother on an Evening in Late Summer" is a
very moving poem, and so is another one about watching
whales being shot by fishermen. That same prolific year, Strand
published one of his most original books. Called *The Monument,*
it is a delightful work, difficult to classify consisting as it does of
fragments, notes on poetry, musings, confessions, and anec-
dotes, which at times read like prose poems. Among other
things, it is a further meditation on time and an address to the
unknown, future reader.

> Though I am reaching over hundreds of years as if they did
> not exist, imagining you at this moment trying to imagine me,
> and proving finally that imagination accomplishes more than
> history, you know me better than I know you. Maybe my voice
> is dim as it reaches over so many years, so many that they seem
> one long blur erased and joined by events and lives that be-
> come one event, one life; even so, my voice is sufficient to
> make *The Monument* out of this moment.

This is an old theme in poetry. Two thousand years ago,
Horace in his poem "Monument" bragged that his verses
would outlast the pyramids. For Strand, too, at the heart of
every poem an appeal to a future reader takes place. His book
The Monument satirizes the dream of literary immortality with
its monstrous narcissism together with the poignant wish of
every human being not to be forgotten. "The secret of human
life," he says, "the universal secret, the root secret from which

all other secrets spring, is the longing for more life." The odds are not very good, as Strand knows well. "O most unhappy Monument! The giant of nothingness [is] rising in sleep," he writes. "O happy Monument! The giant of nothing is taking you with him!"

In *The Continuous Life* (1990), and in the book-length poetic sequence *Dark Harbor* (1993), Strand attempted to enlarge his repertoire. The comic vision encountered in works like *The Monument* and his collection *Mr. and Mrs. Baby and Other Stories* (1985) is from now on to be found in many of his poems. On one hand, he continues to perfect a kind of philosophical lyric on the subject of time and memory, and, on the other, he writes humorous poems, Borgesian prose narratives, slapstick ballads, and satires. I must admit that I prefer Strand at his gloomiest, while realizing that if not for his buffoonery and his self-deprecating tone he would be very hard to take in long stretches. Occasionally, these two divergent impulses come together, as in this wise little poem:

The Idea

For us, too, there was a wish to possess
Something beyond the world we knew, beyond ourselves,
Beyond our power to imagine, something nevertheless
In which we might see ourselves; and this desire
Came always in passing, in waning light, and in such cold
That ice on the valley's lakes cracked and rolled,
And blowing snow covered what earth we saw,
And scenes from the past, when they surfaced again,
Looked not as they had, but ghostly and white
Among false curves and hidden erasures;
And never once did we think we were close
Until the night wind said, "Why do this,
Especially now? Go back to the place you belong;"
And there appeared, with its windows glowing, small,
In the distance, in the frozen reaches, a cabin;
And we stood before it, amazed at its being there,
And would have gone forward and opened the door,
And stepped into the glow and warmed ourselves there,
But that it was ours by not being ours,
And should remain empty. That was the idea.

This is a sad and funny poem. The entire history of American nature poetry is replayed here with its unremitting longing for a grand transcendental vision that would be a revelation of the supreme truth, and a kind of sweet homecoming to the primordial house of our being. There are no lasting "epiphanies," however, in Strand's poetry. At best, there may be only small intimations here and there. In his book on Hopper, while praising the painter for making the most familiar scenes appear remote and enigmatic, he goes on to say: "It is as if we were spectators at an event we were unable to name. We feel the presence of what is hidden, of what surely exists but is not revealed." I believe Strand is convinced that this is as far as we ever get in our knowledge of reality. We may have occasional teasing hints of something else beyond appearances, but no larger view of things.

"Why plug away at the same old self?" Strand asks in *Blizzard of One* (1998). Why, indeed? His answer, I believe, would be that we have no choice. Emily Dickinson scrutinized the goings-on of her inner life in most of the 1,775 poems she wrote in her lifetime and got away with it. The self is the supreme ineffable for both of them. At the heart of their being there is an otherness that transcends language, an unknown that they cannot name. The best poets always turn out to be the ones who fail at what they strive all their lives to say. For over thirty years, Strand has staked everything on that premise. In a few poems in *Blizzard of One,* he makes a further try. A masterly villanelle, an homage to Giorgio de Chirico's enigmatic painting *The Philosopher's Conquest,* ends up being an homage to the poet's own melancholy, the source of his most authentic poems. Like poetry itself, the villanelle tells the story of the eternal return of the same, the same which always turns up a little different, if we have our eyes wide open, and even more so if they are closed in reverie.

The Philosopher's Conquest

This melancholy moment will remain,
So, too, the oracle beyond the gate
And always the tower, the boat, the distant train.

Somewhere in the south a Duke is slain,
A war is won. Here, it is too late.
This melancholy moment will remain.

Here, an autumn evening without rain,
Two artichokes abandoned on a crate,
And always the tower, the boat, the distant train.

Is this another scene of childhood pain?
Why do the clockhands say 1:28?
This melancholy moment will remain.

The green and yellow light of love's domain
Falls upon the joylessness of fate,
And always the tower, the boat, the distant train.

The things our vision wills us to contain,
The life of objects, their unbearable weight.
This melancholy moment will remain,
And always the tower, the boat, the distant train.

Strand's *Chicken, Shadow, Moon and More* (2000) is a book of lists that at times sound like a collection of one-line poems and at other times like a collection of epigrams. Each list is constructed by a repeated use of a single word—so, for instance, his paradise list includes lines like "The toys of paradise wind themselves" and "The poor in paradise have smaller wings," while the hand list has "The cold hand of snow on the hillside" and "The hand that holds the house of cards." Many of the individual lines do not quite come off, but when they do, they exhilarate by their poetic invention and their eloquence. Strand loves verbal fragments as much as he loves the formal perfection of a villanelle. It is these two contrary passions, one for order and the other for the freedom of the imagination, that define him as a poet. "The shadow of chaos is order," he writes. "Come back, shadow of my youth," he continues. "Shadow me, and tell me where I've been."

Servant of the Dictionary:
On Joseph Brodsky

> To you insane world
> But one reply—I refuse.
> —Marina Tsvetaeva

Poets have two ways of achieving fame in autocratic societies: they can either sing the praises of the men in power, or they can irritate them. In the past, it was the monarch and the clergy they had to watch out for. If they got into hot water, banishment and the promise of eternal damnation were the usual punishment. In our time, ideologues of new utopias, from the Soviet Union to China, turned out to be far more bloodthirsty overseers of poetry. Even in the United States, poetry books with real or imagined erotic and blasphemous content are regularly removed from the shelves of school libraries to please some self-appointed thought policeman.

Still, when it comes to making martyrs out of its poets, no country in the history of the world can compete with Russia. Of course, exile, prison, and violent death have been the fate of millions of its citizens in the last century, so one should not single out the misery of poets. In a place where for almost seventy years there was one and only one official pseudoscientific truth, anyone who insisted on his or her own explanation of reality was in grave danger of being sent to prison. Lyric poetry, that most marginal and seemingly inconsequential of activities, came to be regarded as potentially a form of subversive activity. To put the situation another way, a poem became a moral act, the ethics of

Review of *Collected Poems in English,* by Joseph Brodsky. From the *New York Review of Books,* October 19, 2000.

language in a system where lying every time you opened your mouth was every citizen's sacred duty.

Joseph Brodsky, who was born in 1940 in what was then still called Leningrad and died in New York City in 1996, got into precisely that kind of trouble. He said in a moving memoir of his parents, "I am grateful to my mother and my father not only for giving me life but also for failing to bring up their child as a slave." He paid dearly for it. He left school at the age of fifteen, worked in a factory, in a city morgue, and at a number of other jobs across the Soviet Union, and began writing poetry when he was eighteen. As his finely composed and ideologically improper poems became known in literary circles, he was twice locked up in a mental institution and eventually in 1964 tried and sentenced for the crime of social parasitism to five years of hard labor in a remote village in the far north. He shoveled manure and wrote poems that continued to circulate in manuscript in Russia and eventually abroad. Twenty months later, he was released after an appeal to the authorities by prominent Russian cultural figures. When Brodsky returned to Leningrad, he was a hero to the young, a famous poet, and a public enemy without having yet published any poetry.

Subsequently, the KGB made several attempts to remedy that, offering Brodsky publication in a prestigious journal with the attractive prospect of eventually becoming a member of the Communist literary elite, "the state-bred genus, a cross between a parrot and monkey," as he described it. He turned them down. He would not be bought. He also refused to play the victim. "Other people had to go through much more and had a much harder time of it than I did," he said later. In any case, he continued to be an embarrassment to the regime, a free man who said and wrote what he thought and would not be intimidated. Finally, in 1972, he was forcibly expelled from the Soviet Union and came to the United States where, fifteen years later, to the great annoyance of the people who had sent him packing to what they hoped to be everlasting oblivion, he received the Nobel Prize for literature.

"No matter how abominable your condition may be, try not to blame anything or anybody: history, the state, superiors, race, parents, the phase of the moon, childhood, toilet training, etc.,"

Brodsky wrote. He accepted exile, almost took it in stride. What could be more normal for a Russian than to be made homeless? As far as he was concerned, exile was the metaphysical condition par excellence of the human spirit, permanent and without remedy. It taught one humility—which normally it would take a lifetime to acquire. "If one were to assign the life of an exiled writer a genre, it would have to be tragicomedy," he wrote. Yes, there's something funny about misfortune, even one's own. Tragicomedy is the expression of the exile's recognition of the fundamental messiness of everything. It refuses to have events and lives reduced to a single label. Humor is one of the essential manifestations of a free spirit. Authoritarians of all stripes live in fear that someone is making jokes behind their back. A tragic poet is a nuisance already, but a poet who also laughs is a handful even for an evil empire.

Brodsky's essays and memoirs collected in *Less Than One* (1986) and *On Grief and Reason* (1995), without being so intended, give us an intellectual autobiography of the poet. After he was kicked out of school, "that loafer," as his father used to call him, gave himself a solid education. Brodsky was as cosmopolitan a writer as one can imagine. He was born of Jewish parents in the magnificent former capital of a country whose religion was Eastern Orthodox; the political ideal was absolute power, the alphabet Greek, and the architectural style European. In his essays he is curious, probing, imaginative, alert to ideas and their nuances, always irreverent, always opinionated on everything from tyranny to literature, and often very moving. Even when one vehemently disagrees with him, one cannot help but be impressed by his independence and his intellect, and by the quality of his prose. There's hardly a page in the essays where one doesn't come upon a lovely phrase worth underlining:

When it comes to poetry, every bourgeois is a Plato.

The real history of consciousness starts with one's first lie.

For in real tragedy, it is not the hero who perishes: it is the chorus.

Many of his essays, as is to be expected, are about the poets Brodsky admired most, with pointed commentaries on the poems of Auden, Frost, Cavafy, Mandelstam, Tsvetaeva, Rilke, Horace, and Akhmatova. Missing conspicuously are the French poets, the great precursors of Modernism: Baudelaire, Rimbaud, and Mallarmé. Apart from Auden, the European and American avant-garde and its principal figures and ideas are passed over in silence. This is not really surprising. Modernism, with its wholesale rejection of tradition, its firm belief that a poet's cultural inheritance has lost its authority, could not have great appeal for a poet in a country where that inheritance had been made suspect for political reasons and driven underground. In addition, many members of the avant-garde throughout the world supported Stalin and failed to raise their voices in defense of Russian poets who were being persecuted. Some of the greatest names in Russian literature were imprisoned, sent to labor camps, and shot while some of their Western counterparts, particularly in France, wrote poems idealizing their executioners and lived happily ever after.

Modernism's most scandalous notion is that it is possible to begin from scratch and be entirely original as if in the arts everything remains in doubt and awaits discovery. Brodsky, on the other hand, was pretty sure that aesthetic values endure, that a poet who wrote centuries ago is still our contemporary. Indeed, what links the past with the present are poets, the custodians of tradition, who confer with their predecessors as if they were still among us. Pindar, Ovid, and Villon are not only worth reading but also worth emulating. Brodsky wanted poetry to have innumerable voices, rich and dense as the heart of a bustling city. Poetry, for him, was the place where true history was written. History, as historians practice it, looks for reasons; poetry's interest is the human smell of the past. As for culture, when all has been said about it, its real task may be to provide us with the consolation for our mortality.

Brodsky had no use for the free verse tradition of European and American poetry. In an essay on Mandelstam he wrote:

Russian poetry has set an example of moral purity and firmness, which to no small degree has been reflected in the preservation of so-called classical forms without any damage to content. Herein lies her distinction from her Western sisters, though in no way does one presume to judge whom this distinction favors most. However, it is a distinction, and if only for purely ethnographic reasons, that quality ought to be preserved in translation and not forced into some common mold.

This and similar pronouncements, of course, did not make him popular with some American poets.

He once told me seriously that American poets of the generation of Williams, Stevens, Moore, and others ought to have imitated Thomas Hardy. "Had T. S. Eliot, for instance, at the time he read Laforgue," Brodsky wrote, "read Thomas Hardy instead (as I believe Robert Frost did), the history of poetry in English in this century, or to say the least its present, might be somewhat more absorbing." He refused to accept the possibility that American and English literatures had diverged long ago, that sounding like Hardy or Tennyson while living in Brooklyn or Iowa would have seemed outlandish and worthy of ridicule.

That American poets en masse abandoned rhyme and meter did not make sense to Brodsky since ideal verse forms already existed. The prevalent belief that there is a form appropriate to every individual poem must have struck him as nonsense. Nor did he accept the related view that the old poetic idiom in English was inadequate and that its language had grown stale. He would point out the example of Frost, of whom he approved, forgetting that Frost was in no way representative. If one were a budding young poet in New York City seventy years ago, the language and imagery of Eliot and Williams would have reflected far better what one saw and heard every day as one rode the subway to work.

Collected Poems in English represents only a third of Brodsky's poetic work in Russian. Not included is his first book in English, *Selected Poems* (1973), translated by George L. Kline, which includes his early masterpiece "Elegy for John Donne." According to the publisher, it will be reissued later in an expanded edition together with a volume of additional poems translated by other hands. What we have under review then are translations Brodsky himself made, the ones he supervised and gave his approval, plus the poems he wrote in English. Brodsky's output in Russian is large and of the highest quality. In it the breadth of formal invention and rhetorical complexity is staggering. He wrote just about every kind of poem, including long lyrical sequences, dramatic monologues, narratives, odes, elegies, sonnets, and sundry light verse. Modulating levels of diction, playful, witty, and endlessly inventive, he is a mouthful in the original Russian, as anybody who has heard him read can testify. His poems, as with most Russian poetry, have meter and rhyme. Despite the difficulties, of which he was well aware, he insisted throughout his life that they both be faithfully preserved in translations of his work:

> It should be remembered that verse meters in themselves are kinds of spiritual magnitudes for which nothing can be substituted. They cannot be replaced by each other, let alone by free verse. Differences in meters are differences in breath and in heart-beat. Differences in rhyming pattern are those of brain functions. The cavalier treatment of either is at best sacrilege, at worst a mutilation or a murder. In any case, it is a crime of the mind, for which its perpetrator—especially if he is not caught—pays with the price of his intellectual degradation. As for the readers, they buy a lie.

These are very strong words. A demand for fidelity and near-complete identity between the original and the translation is an impossible task to achieve and a prescription for disaster, as he himself admitted at times. He said in an interview:

> It is easier to translate from English into Russian than the reverse. It's just simpler. If only because grammatically Russian is much more flexible. In Russian you can always make up what's been omitted, say just about anything you like. Its power is in subordinate clauses, in all those participial phrases and other grammatical turns of speech that the devil himself could break his leg on. All of this simply does not exist in English. In English translation, preserving this charm is, well, if not impossible, then at least incredibly difficult. So much is lost. Even a good, talented, brilliant poet who intuitively understands the task is incapable of restoring a Russian poem in English. The English language simply doesn't have

those moves. The translator is tied grammatically, structurally. This is why translation from Russian into English always involves straightening the text.

This is perfectly true. Brodsky is without a doubt a great Russian poet, and so are Tsvetaeva, Mandelstam, Pasternak, and Akhmatova, but often one would not know that for certain from the available translations of their work. This is an unusual situation in that we can get a fairly good idea of Apollinaire's or Lorca's greatness without knowing French or Spanish. Even ancient Chinese poets come across in English better than Russians do. As Brodsky said of Horace, whom he could not read in the original, one is "reduced to judging the stuff by the quality of imagination." Could this mean that the quintessential quality of Russian poetry, what makes it different from all other poetries in the world, is its inextricable and untranslatable mixture of sound and meaning? Reading Tsvetaeva or Khlebnikov in the original I certainly have come to believe so. On the other hand, I can also think of a lot of poems of Stevens and Crane whose translation is unimaginable.

"We all work for a dictionary," Brodsky said of the poets. He meant that the Muse is not some nebulous female presence, but a thick, dog-eared book lying on the table. He also said, "In order to write verses you have to stew in the idiomatics of the language constantly." I agree. However, the thicker the stew, the harder it is for the translator to duplicate the recipe. Images and figures of speech can be translated and equivalents found for idioms, but the sound of a mother tongue, its music and what that music evokes in the native reader, cannot be brought over from one language to another. The earlier translations in *Collected Poems* are the work of such well known poets as Richard Wilbur, Anthony Hecht, Derek Walcott, and Howard Moss, who, not knowing Russian, were given literal translations and despite the odds, usually with Brodsky's collaboration, made out of them such good poems that his reputation in this country and England was established straightaway.

It's worth looking closely at how Brodsky himself went about translating his poems. Here is a poem of his I admire in Russian, although I cannot say the same for his English version:

May 24, 1980

I have braved, for want of wild beasts, *steel* cages,
carved my term and nickname on *bunks* and *rafters,*
lived by the sea, *flashed* aces *in an oasis,*
dined with the-devil-knows-whom, in tails, *on truffles.*
From the height of a glacier I beheld half a world, *the earthly*
width. Twice have drowned, *thrice let knives rake my*
nitty-gritty. Quit the country that bore and nursed me.
Those who forgot me would make a city.
I have waded the steppes that saw yelling Huns *in saddles,*
worn clothes nowadays back in fashion *in every quarter,*
planted rye, tarred the roofs of pigsties and stables,
guzzled everything save dry water.
I've admitted the *sentries' third eye into my wet and foul*
dreams. Munched the bread of exile: *it's stale and warty.*
Granted my lungs all sounds except the howl;
switched to a whisper. Now I am forty.
What should I say about life? That it's long *and abhors*
transparence. Broken eggs make me grieve; the omelet, though,
    makes me vomit.
Yet until brown clay has been crammed down my larynx,
only gratitude will be gushing from it.

The words and lines I have made italic are either not in the orig-
inal or, if they are, have been completely reworded with mixed
results. For instance, line 3 of the original reads, "lived by the
sea, played roulette." There are no "truffles" in the original, no
"earthly width," no "knives rake my nitty-gritty." The original
says simply, "Thrice drowned, twice was ripped open." The line
about broken eggs reads, "Only with grief do I feel solidarity."
These paddings serve to keep the meter and rhymes, but they
sacrifice the elegant conciseness and the emotional impact of
the poem in Russian. Some of his substitutions are amusing, like
"flashed aces in an oasis," but others sound unidiomatic and just
awkward. Brodsky has perfect pitch in Russian, but this cannot
be said of many of his translations and of the poems he wrote in
English. They feel for the most part contrived. This is not always
the case, of course, and the originality of Brodsky's poetry can
still come through. But it's obvious to anyone reading him in
both languages that he can be deaf to nuances of usage in his

adopted one. Even his heartbreaking final poem in *Collected Poems*, "Taps," suffers from a number of unfortunate word choices and forced rhymes. I cannot imagine his editors and American poet friends not pointing this out to him. Most likely, he did not take their advice.

> I've been reproached for everything save the weather
> and in turn my own neck was seeking a scimitar.
> But soon, I'm told, I'll lose my epaulets altogether
> and dwindle into a little star.
>
> I'll twinkle among the wires, a sky's lieutenant,
> and hide in clouds when thunder roars,
> blind to the troops as they fold their pennant
> and run, pursued by the pen, in droves.
>
> With nothing around to care for, it's of no import
> if you're blitzed, encircled, reduced to nil.
> Thus wetting his dream with the tumbled ink pot,
> a schoolboy can multiply as no tables will.
>
> And although the speed of light can't in nature covet
> thanks, non-being's blue armor plate,
> prizing attempts at making a sifter of it,
> might use my pinhole, at any rate.

The ideal translation of Brodsky, I imagine, would require a collaborative effort of John Donne, Lord Byron, T. S. Eliot, and W. H. Auden. Here, for instance, are two stanzas from Auden's "Letter to Lord Byron" that may give an idea of Brodsky's wit and deftness in Russian:

> I'm writing this in pencil on my knee,
> Using my other hand to stop me yawning,
> Upon a primitive, unsheltered quay
> In the small hours of a Wednesday morning.
> I cannot add the summer day is dawning;
> In Seythisfjördur every schoolboy knows
> That daylight in the summer never goes.
>
> To get to sleep in latitudes called upper
> Is difficult at first for Englishmen.
> It's like being sent to bed before your supper

For playing darts with father's fountain-pen,
Or like returning after orgies, when
Your breath's like luggage and you realize
You've been more confidential than was wise.

This is an old routine. The Provençal poets pretended to write in a saddle, the Romantics on the bare backs of their sleeping mistresses, the Beats scribbled in back seats of cars speeding across America: the poet as a diarist in a hurry. He jots down what he sees, reports local gossip, dazzles us with his elaborate conceits and metaphors, talks about everything from erotic adventures to God, thinks up rhymes without breaking into a sweat. Here are two stanzas of Brodsky's "The End of a Beautiful Era" in a translation by David Rigsbee and the poet himself:

Since the stern art of poetry calls for words, I, morose,
deaf, and balding ambassador of a more or less
insignificant nation that's stuck in this super
power, wishing to spare my old brain,
hand myself my own topcoat and head for the main
street: to purchase the evening paper. . . .

Everything in these parts is geared for winter: long dreams,
prison walls, overcoats, bridal dresses of whiteness that seems
snowlike. Drinks. Kinds of soap matching dirt in dark corners.
Sparrow vests, second hand of the watch round your wrist,
puritanical mores, underwear. And, tucked in the violinists'
palms, old redwood hand warmers.

Brodsky is the great poet of travel. Perhaps only Allen Ginsberg roamed as much as he did and wrote about it. A poet who gets around has to be able to describe what he sees, and Brodsky is unsurpassed in his ability to evoke the feel of a place. He has poems about London, Venice, Vilna, Mexico City, Florence, Berlin, San Francisco, Belfast, Delphi, Lisbon, Rome; and they are some of his best. He is at his most eloquent in old cities, where the timeless and the transitory come together, where various historical periods live their afterlife side by side. He is their master elegist, the one paying homage and refining the poetic idiom of his predecessors. Wherever he happens to find himself, memories of other worlds pursue him. Brodsky's cross is his uncontainable historical imagination, his ability to see analogies where others do not suspect them. He wanted to be a universal poet, someone at home everywhere, and he largely succeeded. Here's the beginning of one of his finest poems, the twelve-part "Lullaby of Cape Cod," in Anthony Hecht's marvelous translation:

> The eastern tip of the Empire dives into night;
> cicadas fall silent over some empty lawn;
> on classic pediments inscriptions dim from the sight
> as a finial cross darkens and then is gone
> like the nearly empty bottle on the table.
> From the empty street's patrol car a refrain
> of Ray Charles's keyboard tinkles away like rain.
>
> Crawling to a vacant beach from the vast wet
> of ocean, a crab digs into sand laced with sea lather
> and sleeps. A giant clock on a brick tower
> rattles its scissors. The face is drenched with sweat.
> The streetlamps glisten in the stifling weather,
> formally spaced,
> like white shirt buttons open to the waist.
>
> It's stifling. The eye's guided by a blinking stoplight
> in its journey to the whiskey across the room
> on the nightstand. The heart stops dead a moment, but its
>   dull boom
> goes on, and the blood, on pilgrimage gone forth,
> comes back to a crossroad. The body, like an upright,
> rolled-up road map, lifts an eyebrow in the North.

Despite their backdrop of history, Brodsky's poems are immersed in the present. Like his beloved Frost, he's primarily a poet of existential terror. "Because watches keep ticking," he writes in "Lullaby of Cape Cod," and because one's life, of course, is a part of that ticking, one has little choice in the matter. Time, the voiceless, needs a poet's mouth. A poem, that paradox of motion and stillness, makes time speak. Whoever reads a poem overhears someone's dialogue with his mortality. It's possible, however, to make one's fate a part of a bigger story. Most poets can't pull it off. Only a few, and Brodsky is certainly one of them, are able to include in that dialogue the story of their times. Their wish is to be historical witnesses, and their hope is that we recognize ourselves in their words.

In "Lullaby of Cape Cod" one can almost hear the poet breathe with difficulty. It is a stifling night. In a small apartment at the ocean's edge, alone and sleepless, he is mulling over his strange life, where he came from, where he's going, the vastness of this other Empire he exchanged for the old one, the mute, infinite heavens over it, and his own minuteness in comparison. Brodsky was a man of uncommon personal courage and integrity. He did not want to be fooled even by his own rhetoric. He is going for broke, since what he wants is to fully understand his predicament, and follow that knowledge to its bitter end with its thoughts of death and nothingness. He conveys the exhilaration of such moments of clarity, their strangeness and visionary quality:

> a cockroach mob in the stadium
> of the zinc washbasin, crowding around the old
> corpse of a dried-up sponge. Turning its crown,
> a bronze faucet, like Caesar's laureled head,
> deposes upon the living and the dead
> a merciless column of water in which they drown.

Even with the serious problems of translation, there's still plenty of fine poetry in Brodsky's *Collected Poems in English*.

James Merrill and the Spirits

1

The most admiring reader is liable to let out a groan after read-
ing thousands of lines of Wordsworth, Whitman, or Pound over
a short period of time. What at onset is an original style and a
work of genius ends up being a collection of new clichés. De-
spite such risk of exhaustion and disappointment, there's really
no better way to get to know a poet.

In James Merrill's case, there is a surprise awaiting the reader
already on the first page of his *Collected Poems.* One has every
reason to expect, as is usually the case, that the youthful poems
of any poet are bound to be fairly mediocre. It is absolutely
amazing how many great poets started as seemingly talentless
half-wits. Not James Merrill. *First Poems,* published in 1951 in an
edition of only one hundred copies, many of its poems written
as early as 1945, exhibits many of the virtues of his mature style:
a breathtaking ability to handle the most intricate forms and
rhyme schemes, and to do so with apparent ease. The poems are
ornate, dense, obscure, and very literary. Wallace Stevens is
clearly a major influence, and so are the French Symbolist poets
Mallarmé and Baudelaire. Merrill's early poems read like virtu-
oso performances by a prodigy who still hasn't discovered that
there is life outside literature. What seems to be of primary con-
cern to this young poet is the creation of a sensibility in the
process of refining a limited number of strategies within a long
lyrical tradition. This poetry with no hint of the America of the

Review of *Collected Poems,* ed. J. D. McClatchy and Stephen Yenser, and
Familiar Spirits, by Alison Lurie. From the *New York Review of Books,* April
12, 2001.

1940s, one needs to be reminded, was written by an ex-GI. It's as odd and improbable as seeing a performance of an opera at a country fair.

Still, despite the feeling of self-indulgent aestheticism, the opening poem in *Collected Poems*, "The Black Swan," only slightly revised years later, is in my view one of the poet's masterpieces. It is worth quoting in full:

> Black on flat water past the jonquil lawns
> Riding, the black swan draws
> A private chaos warbling in its wake,
> Assuming, like a fourth dimension, splendor
> That calls the child with white ideas of swans
> Nearer to that green lake
> Where every paradox means wonder.
>
> Though the black swan's arched neck is like
> A question-mark on the lake,
> The swan outlaws all possible questioning:
> A thing in itself, like love, like submarine
> Disaster, or the first sound when we wake;
> And the swan-song it sings
> Is the huge silence of the swan.
>
> Illusion: the black swan knows how to break
> Through expectation, beak
> Aimed now at its own breast, now at its image,
> And move across our lives, if the lake is life,
> And by the gentlest turning of its neck
> Transform, in time, time's damage;
> To less than a black plume, time's grief.
>
> Enchanter: the black swan has learned to enter
> Sorrow's lost secret center
> Where like a maypole separate tragedies
> Are wound about a tower of ribbons, and where
> The central hollowness is that pure winter
> That doesn't change but is
> Always brilliant ice and air.
>
> Always the black swan moves on the lake; always
> The blond child stands to gaze
> As the tall emblem pivots and rides out

To the opposite side, always. The child upon
The bank, hands full of difficult marvels, stays
Forever to cry aloud
In anguish: I love the black swan.

Merrill was then and continued to be the poet of a troubled
childhood. He was the only child of Charles Edward Merrill, a
founder of the highly successful brokerage firm Merrill Lynch,
and his second wife, Hellen Ingram, who came from a socially
prominent family in Jacksonville, Florida. His parents divorced
when he was thirteen years old. He grew up lonely, raised pri-
marily by a French governess in an atmosphere of enormous
wealth in New York, Palm Beach, and Southampton, Long Is-
land. In "The Black Swan," he reminds me of another solitary
child, the one in Arthur Rimbaud's "The Drunken Boat," whom
we discover at the end of the poem to be the originator of the
fabulous voyages the poem has just described. He is the one
floating a small paper boat in a cold puddle in the street.

That vulnerable, dreaming child, who relives a moment of ter-
ror or happiness, is the hero of many of Merrill's poems. "I love
the black swan," the boy says. What he loves is the self-enclosed,
beautiful world his imagination has constructed. "Poets convince
us that all our childhood reveries are worth starting again," Gas-
ton Bachelard wrote.[1] Merrill certainly did that. What is remark-
able to me about this poem is how the reality of that child's soli-
tude nevertheless breaks through the artifice. The poem is both
poignant and prophetic. Merrill would write many others about
his childhood in search of a key to the secret of his identity and
the sources of his poetic vision.

There's a general agreement that with *Water Street* (1962) and
succeeding volumes, Merrill's poetry changes for the better. He
leaves behind the aesthete's aloofness of his earlier poetry, that
impression of wanting to dazzle the reader with his quick wit and
nothing terribly urgent at stake. The late 1950s and early 1960s
were the period when so-called Confessional poetry was all the
rage in this country. The poems in Robert Lowell's *Life Studies,*
with their autobiographical bent and shameless self-concentra-
tion, were widely imitated. Merrill's poems, too, begin to sound
more personal, although he does not share Lowell's need to

blurt out dark secrets and appall the reader. He's more reticent, more sneaky, and in his own way more terrifying. Here, for instance, is a section from the sequence "The Broken Home" in *Nights and Days* (1966), which describes a troubling and never to be forgotten encounter with his Medusa-like mother:

> One afternoon, red, satyr-thighed
> Michael, the Irish setter, head
> Passionately lowered, led
> The child I was to a shut door. Inside,
>
> Blinds beat sun from the bed.
> The green-gold room throbbed like a bruise.
> Under a sheet, clad in taboos
> Lay whom we sought, her hair undone, outspread,
>
> And of a blackness found, if ever now, in old
> Engravings where the acid bit.
> I must have needed to touch it
> Or the whiteness—was she dead?
> Her eyes flew open, startled strange and cold.
> The dog slumped to the floor. She reached for me. I fled.

Merrill is both a poet of memory and an epicure of daily life. He speaks approvingly of Eugenio Montale's poetry that is "surprisingly permeable by quite ordinary objects—ladles, hens, pianos, half-read letters." "To me," he continues, "he's the twentieth-century nature poet."[2] This is true of Merrill himself. He's the poet of intimate spaces as much as he is the poet of travel. A cozy room with all its furnishings carefully enumerated, where the comedy of manners unfolds between four walls, is the setting of many of his poems. People gossip, fall in and out of love, grow bored or introspective. It's all very theatrical and very civilized. Then, as on the stage, something out of the ordinary happens. There's a moment of revelation, a small epiphany that transforms the commonplace event:

Charles on Fire

> Another evening we sprawled about discussing
> Appearances. And it was the consensus
> That while uncommon physical good looks

Continued to launch one, as before, in life
(Among its vaporous eddies and false calms),
Still, as one of us said into his beard,
"Without your intellectual and spiritual
Values, man, you are sunk." No one but squared
The shoulders of his own unloveliness.
Long-suffering Charles, having cooked and served the meal,
Now brought out little tumblers finely etched
He filled with amber liquor and then passed.
"Say," said the same young man, "in Paris, France,
They do it this way"—bounding to his feet
And touching a lit match to our host's full glass.
A blue flame, gentle, beautiful, came, went
Above the surface. In a hush that fell
We heard the vessel crack. The contents drained
As who should step down from a crystal coach.
Steward of spirits, Charles's glistening hand
All at once gloved itself in eeriness.
The moment passed. He made two quick sweeps and
Was flesh again. "It couldn't matter less,"
He said, but with a shocked, unconscious glance
Into the mirror. Finding nothing changed,
He filled a fresh glass and sank down among us.

There are a good many equally marvelous poems in Merrill's middle period. I'll mention a few that struck me as being even better than I remembered them: "Hôtel de l'Univers et Portugal," "The Octopus," "Doodler," "The Urban Convalescence," "A Vision of the Garden," "Prism," "For Proust," "Nightgown," "From the Cupola," "Remora," "Days of 1935," "The Victor Dog," and "Lost in Translation." Merrill demands that he be read with extreme care. The poems' pleasures lie in details where his impeccable ear for language, his huge vocabulary, and his play of wit are on display. He can spin a tale, keep the poem going through countless twists and turns of the plot, and hold us spellbound. That extraordinary facility can at times be irritating. One begins to suspect that he can make a poem out of any occasion, no matter how trivial. Merrill admitted that he never learned how to read newspapers, and indeed, his references to contemporary events are infrequent. Even his few New York poems are not particularly vivid for me. That is not where his heart is. His milieu is social, intimate, and domestic. In his fascination with manners throughout the *Collected Poems*, he is as much a satirist as he is a lyric poet.

2

The publication of *The Book of Ephraim* in *Divine Comedies* (1977), the first volume of the trilogy *The Changing Light at Sandover*, broadened his subject matter and attracted considerable attention. Ephraim was a spirit who communicated his revelations and those of other spirits to Merrill and his companion, David Jackson, by way of a Ouija board. What we have then is a poem that in addition to narrative and commentary in verse incorporates transcriptions of actual messages from the other world. The reception was mixed. There were those who like Harold Bloom spoke of "occult splendor in which Merrill rivals Yeats's *A Vision*, Stevens's ghostly *The Owl in the Sarcophagus*, and even some aspects of Proust," and those leery of candlelit séances who simply did not know what to make of it all. That it is the most unusual poem ever written in America, and that its intellectual ambitions are immense, there's no doubt. The controversy regarding the poem has continued and is not about to die down with the publication of the novelist Alison Lurie's memoir about Merrill and Jackson and their twenty-five years of involvement with the Ouija board.

Lurie and Merrill met in the summer of 1950 in Salzburg, Austria, while both were traveling in Europe, but their friendship really began in 1955, when Merrill took a position as a visiting writer at Amherst College, where Lurie's husband was teaching. He arrived accompanied by his new friend David Jackson. Lurie describes Merrill as an elegantly handsome man with impeccable manners he had learned as a child from his mother and his governess. He knew French, German, Italian, modern and classical Greek, and Latin, and could make puns in several languages at once. As she says:

> The 1950s and early 1960s were a good time for David and Jimmy. They were young and in love; they had no economic

worries; they lived in an odd but beautiful house in a picturesque village on the New England coast. When not at home they traveled together round the world and made friends everywhere.

She liked visiting them at their house in Stonington, Connecticut:

> To go to 107 Water Street from a house cluttered with shabby, worn furniture and toys and dirty laundry and the cries of children was like being transported to another world: one not only more attractive, but more luxurious, calm, and voluptuous; more free and leisured—a world in which the highest goods were friendship, pleasure, and art.

As pleasant as their lives were, Lurie became sure of underlying tensions. Jackson, who was also independently well-off, was an unsuccessful fiction writer, the author of a few well-received short stories and five unpublished novels. By 1959, Merrill had already published a short novel, *The Seraglio,* and another book of poems, *The Country of a Thousand Years of Peace.* Throughout the 1950s, from time to time, they would take out the Ouija board to entertain themselves with lighthearted messages, but in September of 1965, they took it up again, this time with great seriousness. On one hand, there was Jackson with his frustrated creative energy and, on the other, Merrill intrigued by the possibility that he might actually have been making contact with the dead. "It is inside that I need to change," he wrote in his own memoir, *A Different Person.* "To this end I hope very diffidently to get away from the kind of poetry I've been writing."

"They didn't suspect," Lurie remarks, "that what started as an evening's amusement would consume so much of their lives over the years to come, how at times it would become so absorbing that reality itself would seem faded, flimsy, and ghostlike." This is the puzzle her memoir tries to solve. It involves a furtive lovers' quarrel between the two while they were ostensibly engaged in a spiritual adventure. In 1976, after over twenty years of intermittent sessions, Merrill decided to make use of the revelations, first in the form of a novel, and eventually in a poem, *The Book of Ephraim,* followed soon after by *Mirabell's Books of Number* (1978) and *Scripts for the Pageant* (1980). All three, with

Coda: The Higher Keys, were published in 1982 as *The Changing Light at Sandover.* The long poem, or so we believe in America, is supposed to be the test of any poet's true powers. "The notion," Merrill wrote in his memoirs, "struck me at twenty—at forty, too, for that matter—as a dangerous form of megalomania, and I wasn't buying any of it. But at fifty? Longer than Dante, dottier than Pound, and full of spirits more talkative than Yeats himself might have wished."

Lurie doesn't think much of the trilogy as metaphysics. She admires the poems in it, but cannot accept its fundamental premise, and neither can I. The claim that a poet is a medium who merely transmits what he has received from some unknown source has been around since the Romantics. However, such inspired moments of automatic writing were thought to be rare. Merrill's immortals in the hereafter, on the other hand, are garrulous. They are not just a poetic conceit, it turns out, but are to be taken seriously. What at first, in *The Book of Ephraim*'s twenty-six poems, has a tongue-in-cheek quality becomes farfetched in later books, where transcriptions of messages in blocks of uppercase letters predominate and Plato, Buddha, Homer, Mohammed, Jesus, and scores of other illustrious names have their say. Merrill and Jackson occasionally hint that they suspect the whole thing is a delightful fabrication, a genie conjured up out of their unconscious selves, and then they seem to forget that.

The abstruse mystical doctrine that purports to explain God and his creation, including such perennial brain-twisters as Atlantis, Stonehenge, the Bermuda Triangle, black holes, and flying saucers—to name only a few—inevitably drowns out the poetry. Merrill's enlightened voices from above are, of course, a familiar phenomenon in our culture, where, as Lurie points out,

> apparently, celebrities from everywhere in the world and over three thousand years of history are eager to communicate with contemporary housewives and small businessmen, secretaries and schoolteachers, teenagers and senior citizens. Egyptian pharaohs and Greek philosophers, European kings and queens and world-renowned writers and artists and musicians crowd into small-town sitting rooms to discuss art, religion, philosophy, and current events.

Imparting wisdom from on high is never an advisable strategy in poetry. Merrill's best poems let the readers' imagination draw out their meanings for themselves. Not here. There are narrative and lyric interludes in the trilogy that rank among some of the liveliest poetry Merrill ever wrote, but they do not salvage the epic from being a largely didactic poem.

"When two sophisticated, extremely intelligent people devote over twenty-five years to recording messages from imaginary beings, you have to ask, What was in it for them?" Lurie writes. As a novelist, she is less interested in angels than in the games her two friends were playing. Her memoir seeks to unearth what was psychologically at stake for the participants. For Merrill, the messages from the spirits were primarily raw material for what was hoped to be a major poem. For Jackson, who is the unacknowledged coauthor of the trilogy and whose experience as a novelist undoubtedly contributed to the creation of its cast of characters, they were a way of sustaining the increasingly complex and destructive relationship with his lover. One may not agree entirely with Lurie's conclusions, but *Familiar Spirits* is an exquisitely written and powerful little book.

3

Merrill is at the top of his form in his later books of poems, *Late Settings* (1985), *The Inner Room* (1988), and *A Scattering of Salts* (1995). The poems, with their accretion of detail, have a novelistic richness. One of Merrill's great talents was always his ability to describe well. About his first visit to Rome as a young man, Merrill says, "A thousand details reached me, but like a primitive painter ignorant of perspective, I had no way to order them; the mosquito was the same size as the horse or the purple blossom of the artichoke." Now he knows how to do it.

Merrill is a poet quivering with awareness, alert to every sight and new sensation in his surroundings as he is to every nuance of language. Again and again, he is the poet of a memorable occasion, of exhilaration and delight some chance event brought to him. Here's one such poem:

Graffito

Deep in weeds, on a smooth chunk of stone
Fallen from the cornice of the church
(Originally a temple to Fortuna),
Appears this forearm neatly drawn in black,
Wearing, lest we misunderstand,
Like a tattoo the cross-within-a-circle
Of the majority—Christian Democrat.

Arms and the man. This arm ends in a hand
Which grasps a neatly, elegantly drawn
Cock—erect and spurting tiny stars—
And balls. One sports . . . a swastika?
Yes, and its twin, if you please, a hammer-and-sickle!
The tiny stars, seen close, are stars of David.
Now what are we supposed to make of that?

Wink from Lorenzo, pout from Mrs. Pratt.
Hold on, I want to photograph this latest
Fountain of Rome, whose twinkling gist
Gusts my way from an age when isms were largely
Come-ons for the priapic satirist,
And any young guy with a pencil felt
He held the fate of nations in his fist.

It's all here: paganism, Catholic religion, fascism, communism, Nazism, and even a hint of anti-Semitism. Long before Freud, the graffiti artists everywhere knew that sex and power go hand in hand. This lucky find is worth photographing like any other tourist attraction in Rome. The poem, too, is a snapshot, so clear one instantly intuits the larger implications of what one has just seen, down to the final jest about the young political visionary holding his pen and presumably also his cock in his fist.

The later poems inevitably have an elegiac and introspective mood. A number of Merrill's close friends had died of AIDS, and he himself was diagnosed as having the virus in 1986, although he kept it a secret. Against such grim reality, the issue in a number of poems, even more than before, is how to recover in small measure and prolong some intensely lived moment. Merrill is still a poet who keeps what at times sounds like a diary in verse, writing poems about his father's Irish setters, scrapping his computer, a dry-out farm, Wagner's Ring cycle at the Met, his mother's pearls, and even his contact lenses. There are many fine poems, among which I particularly admire "Page from the Koran," "The House Fly," "Santo," "Trees Listening to Bach," "The Dresden Doll," "A Room at the Heart of Things," "Walks in Rome," "Snow Jobs," "164 East 72nd Street," and "Self-Portrait in Tyvek™ Windbreaker."

Merrill's poems do not change much over the years. *Collected Poems* ends up being an autobiography of a very private man with a small circle of friends and lovers to whom he remained devoted. There are poets, like Robert Lowell, Elizabeth Bishop, Frank O'Hara, and John Ashbery, who one feels get closer to our complex reality. Merrill is without equal in American poetry when it comes to formal mastery, but despite his considerable range of interests, his take on things may be a bit too mandarin for some tastes. Working within the tradition was his strength and his limitation. He's clever and inventive, but he did not enlarge our idea of what poetry can be as much as these other poets, who took greater risks with the lyric by daring to be antipoetic both in how they wrote their poems and in what they wrote about.

"Art. It cures affliction," Merrill says in a late poem. Poetry staves off the inevitable for him by transforming our sensual experience into an aesthetic one and the aesthetic into a spiritual one. These transmutations, however, cannot be willed. The problem with the *Sandover* trilogy is that it omits one important step. It seeks transcendence without a credible basis in experience. As Stevens cautioned, "The imagination loses vitality as it ceases to adhere to what is real. When it adheres to the unreal and intensifies what is unreal, while its first effect may be extraordinary, the effect is the maximum effect that it will ever have."[3] Merrill is a better poet and a wiser man when he allows the meaning in his poems to come unbidden out of the ingredients at hand, where it lay hidden in some idiom or metaphor. When that happens, as in "An Upward Look," the closing poem in *A Scattering of Salts,* one not only believes in the vision but is also deeply moved:

O heart green acre sown with salt
by the departing occupier

lay down your gallant spears of wheat
Salt of the earth each stellar pinch

flung in blind defiance backwards
now takes its toll Up from this quieted

quarry the lover colder and wiser
hauling himself finds the world turning

toys triumphs toxins into
this vast facility the living come
dearest to die in How did it happen

In bright alternation minutely mirrored
within the thinking of each and every

mortal creature halves of a clue
approach the earthlights Morning star

evening star salt of the sky
First the grave dissolving into dawn

then the crucial recrystallizing
from inmost depths of clear dark blue

"The ancient comic theater had it right," he begins another late poem. He has in mind that "moment comedies beget / when escapade and hubbub die away, / Vows are renewed, masks dropped," and "Nature must do the rest." There was always a conflict in Merrill between giving himself fully over to some all-consuming aesthetic emotion and his ironic detachment. Perhaps it is not surprising that these mixed feelings remained with him to the end of his life. In the previously uncollected poem "Days of 1994," written months before his death, he describes waking in a friend's room, watching the dawn light, an infant sun tottering on stilts of shade through misty greens, while close by a dragonfly shivers. However, it's not only the magician but also the tough realist in Merrill who makes this farewell poem so heart-wrenching. The truth of his poetry turns out to be the stoic truth:

I shiver next, Light walking on my grave . . .
And sleep, and wake. This time, peer out
From just beneath the mirror of the lake
A gentle mile uphill.
Florets—the mountain laurel—float
Openmouthed, devout,
Set swaying by the wake of the flatboat:

Barcarole whose chords of gloom
Draw forth the youngest, purest, faithfullest,
Cool-crystal-casketed
Hands crossed on breast,
Pre-Raphaelite face radiant—and look,
Not dead, O never dead!
To wake, to wake
Among the flaming dowels of a tomb
Below the world, the thousand things
Here risen to if not above
Before day ends:
The spectacles, the book,
Forgetful lover and forgotten love,
Cobweb hung with trophy wings,
The fading trumpet of a car,
The knowing glance from star to star,
The laughter of old friends.

NOTES

1. Gaston Bachelard, *The Poetics of Reverie,* trans. Daniel Russell (Boston: Beacon Press, 1971), p. 105.

2. James Merrill, *Recitative* (San Francisco: North Point Press, 1986), p. 28.

3. Wallace Stevens, *The Necessary Angel* (New York: Knopf, 1951), p. 6.

The Thinking Man's Comedy:
On Saul Bellow

The soul of another is a dark forest.
—Russian saying

It is the voice rather than the plots of Saul Bellow's novels that sticks in my mind. His heroes don't do much. They talk endlessly, mostly to themselves. In long, diverting, and funny monologues they unburden themselves of their troubles in a mix of rough street talk and bookish philosophizing. Like soapbox characters I heard in my youth on Bughouse Square in Chicago, they have hundreds of grievances and hold outrageous opinions on everything from women to the way our country is run. They are brainy, self-absorbed, perpetually fixated on some wrong done to them, and in a constant state of agitation. The basis of Bellow's humor is that the hero is usually someone who has made a complete mess of his life. This has always been the comic writer's view of humanity. Tragic heroes complain only to the gods; the comic ones squabble with their families and dream of settling scores with their real and imaginary enemies.

In Bellow, some of that sense of being a fall guy is undoubtedly the result of the immigrant experience, where it's common to have had a life more absurd than any plot of a picaresque novel. "Mother Herzog," Bellow writes of Herzog's mother,

> had a way of meeting the present with a partly averted face.
> She encountered it on the left but sometimes seemed to
> avoid it on the right. On this withdrawn side she often had a

Review of *Bellow: A Biography,* by James Atlas. From the *New York Review of Books,* May 31, 2001.

dreaming look, melancholy, and seemed to be seeing the Old World—her father the famous *misnagid,* her tragic mother, her brothers living and dead, her sister and her linens and servants in Petersburg, the dacha in Finland (all founded on Egyptian onions). Now she was cook, washerwoman, seamstress on Napoleon Street in the slum. Her hair turned gray, and she lost her teeth, her very fingernails wrinkled. Her hands smelled of the sink.

No one who has been thus set adrift by one of history's practical jokes is a great believer in Reason. One can say anything about history except that it gives a hoot what happens to one person or another. It's tough for anyone to figure out why his or her life turned out the way it did. For an immigrant it becomes almost a metaphysical problem. The absurd is the only reality there is, so for an individual, life is all about luck.

Bellow himself, James Atlas tells us in his biography, was born in 1915 in Lachine, an outskirt of Montreal packed with working-class Russians, Poles, Ukrainians, Greeks, and Italians. He was the fourth child of Jewish parents who had emigrated from Russia two years before he was born. "The trunks my parents traveled with were exotic—the taffeta petticoats, the ostrich plumes, the long gloves, the buttoned boots, and all the rest of those family treasures," Bellow recalled, "made me feel that I'd come from another world." Now they were among millions of new immigrants, having a hard time making ends meet. "A sickly child, afflicted with respiratory ailments, he was his mother's favorite; she treated him like an invalid," Atlas writes. After his father, who in the meantime had become a bootlegger, had a load of booze hijacked at gunpoint and was himself beaten and left in a ditch, the family got in touch with a cousin in Chicago. The father went first, and the mother and the children were smuggled across the United States border in July 1924 by one of the father's underworld associates.

"Give Chicago half a chance, and it will turn you into a philosopher," Bellow wrote. In his youth and for years afterward, it was a smoke-shrouded city of factories and ugly, poverty-stricken neighborhoods smelling of ethnic cooking and of stockyards where death-bound cattle and sheep waited their turn. Along Lake Michigan, where the well-to-do lived, Chicago was like a resort town with beaches, elegant hotels, and expensive stores. Only a few blocks inland, vast slums began with their taverns, pool halls, and flophouses. Raskolnikov would have felt right at home here, I remember thinking when I lived there.

The contrast between Chicago's neighborhoods could have provided fitting illustrations for an edition of *The Communist Manifesto:* the fabulously rich and the masses of working stiffs hustling in a sprawling factory town. Everybody worked side by side with other nationalities, bantering in a mixture of languages so fantastic a professional linguist would have had a hard time describing what he heard. "Rootlessness, so frightening to some, exhilarates others," Bellow said. Identities, which other Americans took for granted, immigrants had to invent from scratch. It took time to grasp that one could make oneself over, that one could become someone else here in America. Immigrants who understood very well that they were regarded as the lowest trash nevertheless knew that "freedom" and "opportunity" were not mere talk, since they could see their material circumstances improve, and for many of them that was all that really mattered.

Still, some of the children of the immigrants were serious readers. When Bellow was in high school, Atlas tells us, the Russian Literary Society met at a hot-dog stand on Division Street. I myself remember encountering more than a few autodidacts, lowly office clerks and manual workers who claimed to have read everything and actually seemed to have done just that. Bellow spent the years of the Great Depression with his nose in a book. The public libraries were well stocked and much used. Years later he recalled the atmosphere:

> The North Avenue Branch, like a church or a school, offered a privileged environment. The books were bound in brown buckram. The pages were stained with soup, or cocoa or tomato ketchup or by tears or by nosebleeds, and they were also fiercely annotated by borrowers. Readers denounced writers or praised them, argued with other readers around the margins—self-made prophets, poets in their own right, patriots, subversives, philosophers, neighborhood historians

arguing the Civil War or the Russian Revolution. One could learn a lot about the mental life of a democracy from these annotations. Strange forms of originality sometimes appeared, special kinds of intelligence, passion and madness.

At the University of Chicago, which Bellow attended before transferring to Northwestern to study anthropology, the curriculum centered on the classics of Western civilization. As for his switch, Atlas writes, "He was a savage himself, he joked; why not study his own kind?" In fact, what he really wanted to be was a writer. His family, as is usually the case, was against it. If he writes books, kick the bum out, is advice as old as the invention of writing. Even at Northwestern, as he neared graduation, he was told by the chairman of the English department to forget about studying literature. "No Jew could really grasp the tradition of English literature," the man explained. One needs to remember how Anglophile our English departments were then. If one spoke with admiration of Dreiser or Frank Norris in my day, one was likely to be pitied as being a yokel.

Even Lionel Trilling declared that this country offered "no opportunity for the novelist to do his job of searching out reality." I myself was told by a professor in Chicago to stop wasting my time reading Walt Whitman and read Thomas Hardy instead. My fellow poets, on the other hand, urged me to forget about Robert Lowell and the rest of those Boston and New York phonies. It was a quarrel between two sets of provincials, those who believed that the "real" America was right here in Chicago and those who behaved as if culturally we were still a British colony. Bellow, who never forgot a put-down, continued to distrust the academy and the literary establishment all his life as if he were still an outsider.

Immigrants can turn out to be the ultimate subversives. No wonder that nationalists everywhere rage against them when they are not killing them. In time, immigrants may sneak both their cooking and their humor into the mainstream culture. They may enrich the language. It's been said again and again that Bellow gave new life to American literature by bringing Jewish experience and its verbal wit into American fiction, and it is still worth saying. The "Europeanization of American literature" is what the critic Philip Rahv called it, and this had nothing to do with the usual academic adulation of London and Paris. Bellow gave the realist novel of Dreiser and Farrell a new twist by mixing in Chekhov, Babel, Joyce, and even Céline. He wanted a novel that could be many things at the same time, earthy and philosophical, colloquial and literary, with plenty of room for buffoonery along the way.

Even the best of biographies can be both enjoyable and exasperating. The general rule seems to be, the more one knows about someone's life, the more impatient and judgmental one is about him or her. Since we all have plenty of troubles of our own, other people's failings, spelled out at great length, tend to get tiresome. I realize this is not universally true. Devotees of afternoon soaps can spend twenty years happily captivated by the ceaseless turns of fortune of some character. For me, it's an aesthetic issue. I like literary works where economy and the sense of form are highly valued, while in biography the ideal seems to be a ten-act opera. I don't wish to give the impression that Atlas's book is not worth reading. It is very much so, but it could have been cut down considerably. As is often the case, the recreation of the historical period ends up being more interesting than the life being told. When it comes to description and anecdotes, the more detail the better. The first seventy pages of Atlas's biography, with their marvelous evocation of the Montreal and Chicago of Bellow's youth, and a number of other stretches in the book describing postwar New York and its intellectual circles, are fascinating to read.

Bellow certainly is not an easy subject to get hold of. He's a complex character, perhaps better suited for fiction than for biography. As the old blues song goes, he had more women than a passenger train can hold. For a biographer that can be a trap because it invites him to sort out the guilty from the innocent parties in all these relationships. Married five times, four times divorced with plenty of infidelities on the side, Bellow made excuses for himself in his novels while blackening the reputation of his women. That's the trouble one gets in when one bases characters in one's books on real people. The biographer, no matter how much he cautions himself against such simpleminded readings, nevertheless reads the novels as if they were autobiography and not fiction. These wives simply could not all have been as bad as Bellow depicts them, Atlas thinks, and who would disagree?

Unfortunately, he comes to a conclusion. No biographer simply throws up his hands and says, I have no idea what to make of this fellow. I myself often wish they would do that. Instead, Atlas psychoanalyzes Bellow and thinks he has discovered what he has been repressing, namely his lifelong guilt over his inattention to his mother at the time of her dying. There's more, and it gets worse. Bellow, in Atlas's account, is a bad friend. He is a lousy lover. He may be a closet homosexual and a racist. He is a master of self-exculpation. He is a sucker for flattery. In his books, he gives us idealized versions of himself while running away from deeper truths of his life.

For me, the question is not whether Atlas is right or wrong about any of this, but rather whether there is a human being anywhere who would come off very well after a close scrutiny of every aspect of his or her life. The Catholic church is careful when it comes to bestowing sainthood on anyone, at times taking centuries to sort out all the evidence. Its message is clear. Most of us are sinners; we only differ in degree. When that truth is lost on a biographer, who to his surprise and shock repeatedly discovers that the man he is writing about is flawed, much of his narrative becomes an exercise in futility. In the end, the failures of the subject make the biographer feel morally superior, which is a ridiculous position to find oneself in. As far as I'm concerned, those failings are mostly beside the point. Great works of literature have been written with the basest of motives by despicable human beings. I wonder how many biographies have turned the literary admirers of authors against them.

I have other complaints. For example, Bellow is interested in all kinds of ideas, and his biographer is far less so. In fact, Atlas regards the presence of ideas in novels as no more than showing off by the author, whose purpose is to impress the gullible reader with his seriousness:

Philosophy, then and later, was one of the unfortunate legacies of Bellow's immersion in the University of Chicago Great Books culture. His heroes shared a penchant for belaboring ideas. They were the products of a provincial Chicago boy's effort to show that he wasn't provincial, that he was at home with the whole of Western thought; unconsciously, perhaps, they expressed an impulse to distance himself from his true and more painful material—a flight into abstraction.

At its best, the habitual philosophizing of Bellow's characters was a marvelous satirical tool. Moses Herzog's elaborate disquisitions on Romanticism and phenomenology, Charlie Citrine's meditations on death and the immortality of the soul, were meant to be funny, Bellow plaintively reminded critics who took him too seriously (though these speculative flights also provided a showcase for his erudition).

Certainly, satire is part of the intention, but Bellow's ideas are not just there for laughs. "One of the most striking features of Bellow's work," Atlas rightly notes elsewhere in his biography, "is its refusal to be bound by the conventional definitions of what constitutes literary seriousness." Bellow likes the mix of high and low sentiments. Nevertheless, he has a good nose for ideas that matter. One of the pleasures of his novels is the company of a restless mind skipping from subject to subject, keenly aware of intellectual history down to its contemporary trends and quite capable of contributing an original insight now and then. His eyes work well, and so does his intellect. In fact, one cannot separate the two. If ideas were just a bit of window dressing, the novels would have no dramatic impact and they would not even be funny. Here is how he describes the predicament of his hero in *Herzog:*

> The description might begin with his wild internal disorder, or even with the fact that he was quivering. And why? Because he let the entire world press upon him. For instance? Well, for instance, what it means to be a man. In a city. In a century. In transition. In a mass. Transformed by science. Under organized power. Subject to tremendous controls. In a condition caused by mechanization. After the late failure of radical hopes. In a society that was no community and devalued the person. Owing to the multiplied power of numbers which made the self negligible. Which spent military billions against foreign enemies but would not pay for order at home. Which permitted savagery and barbarism in its own great cities. At

the same time, the pressure of human millions. . . . Would you deny them the right to exist? Would you ask them to labor and go hungry while you enjoyed delicious old-fashioned Values?

Bellow's genius is that he makes us recognize ourselves even in his most outlandish characters. We can identify with some of his heroes once we realize that intellectually we are in the same pickle they are in. I have in mind the difficulties any thinking person has in a world such as ours, which has no use for independent thinking. When one adds that his heroes are usually members of one beleaguered minority after another, the habitual suspicion and the caustic wit make it even harder to decide what to believe in. In the case of Bellow, who conceived of fiction as a higher form of autobiography, it comes down to the basic questions of who I am and what I live for. As he said in a lecture:

> But of course the prevailing assumption—and the Romantic assumption still prevailed—was that man could find the true meaning of life and of his own unique being by separating himself from society and its activities and collective illusions. If walking on the mountains as a solitary Rousseau didn't turn the trick, you could go and derange your senses artificially, as Rimbaud recommended.

Not Bellow. He knows backwards and forwards all the ways our spiritual and mental doctors have devised to pull wool over everybody's eyes. His heroes suffer from many things, but above all from knowing too much. They cannot bring themselves to give credence to one idea for very long, so they thrive as best as they can in the midst of monstrous contradictions. It's like being a lifelong atheist and believing in every superstition at the same time. They know it's absurd, so they rant. "The human mind is not a dignified organ," Bellow quotes E. M. Forster with approval. The inventory of a consciousness at any given time makes a joke of any ideal conception of human beings. That's the state of affairs of which he keeps reminding his readers.

One minute consumed with some pettiness, the next minute addressing a lofty ethical question—if the voice one encounters in his novels has a literary precursor, it is the nameless narrator of Dostoevsky's *Notes from Underground*. Like Bellow's heroes, he is self-conscious to an extreme degree and is at the mercy of the constant turmoil inside him. Everywhere he turns in his mind he encounters himself, so there's little we can say about him that he already has not anticipated. It's because he suspects others are watching him and thinking about him that he strives to keep one step ahead of them by imagining what that may be. In the meantime, he's trying to explain himself to himself, justify his actions, and find loopholes to outwit the harsh judgment he has already passed on himself. His mental state is one of pervasive indignation at everyone and everything. He is torn between the conviction that one's character determines all one's actions, that one is not free and never was, and the contrary feeling that everything within oneself is still open and undetermined. In the end, he can do very little. He's stuck with the paralyzing thought that an intelligent man cannot seriously become anything, that only a fool and a crook can become something. Bellow, too, is convinced that to have a conscience is, after a certain age, to live permanently in an epistemological hell. The reason his and Dostoevsky's heroes are incapable of ever arriving at any closure is that they love their own suffering above everything else. They refuse to exchange their inner torment for the peace of mind that comes with bourgeois propriety or some kind of religious belief. In fact, they see their suffering as perhaps the last outpost of the heroic in our day and age.

Rereading many of the novels, as I did for this review, I was reminded how good the best of them are. Bellow is a supremely entertaining writer not only because he writes beautiful prose but also because he's always topical. Whatever intellectual fashion was all the rage at the time of the writing is dissected in the novels. In addition, he is extraordinarily observant. His books abound in luminous details of the physical world. Seeing for Bellow is the supreme sensual pleasure. If one wishes to know what it was like to walk the streets of Chicago and New York in the second half of the twentieth century, one ought to read him. His best descriptive passages combine the clarity and mystery of great black-and-white photographs of the 1930s and 1940s. Walker Evans, Helen Levitt, David Vestal, and Louis Stettner come to mind, except photographs are mute. Here's a passage from his novel *Ravelstein* that reads like one of Baudelaire's prose poems:

> On Roy Street in Montreal a dray horse has fallen down on the icy pavement. The air is as dark as a gray coat-lining. A smaller animal might have found its feet, but this beast with its huge haunches could only work his hoofs in the air. The long-haired Percheron with startled eyes and staring veins will need a giant to save him, but on the corner a crowd of small men can only call out suggestions. They tell the cop he's lucky the horse fell on Roy Street, easier to write in his report than Lagauchettierre. Then there is a strange and endless procession of schoolgirls marching by twos in black uniform dresses. Their faces white enough to be tubercular. The nuns who oversee them keep their hands warm within their sleeves. The puddles in this dirt street are deep and carry a skim of ice.

If Bellow has a recurring theme—and he does—it's the unhappy family. The family, the institution our conservatives like to wax lyrical about, is without doubt the place of both our greatest joys and our lasting miseries. Parents and children fight, and so do husbands and wives. Bellow's novels offer countless examples of how people who love each other descend into hatred. There's usually a selfless aunt or a grandfather who rises above the endless bickering and is a figure long remembered and cherished, but the rest of what happens in families is all tooth and claw. Bellow's leading characters generally do not get on well with women. They are convinced that their wives are out to destroy them. "Wisdom, beauty, glory, courage in men are just vanities and her business is to beat down the man's legends about himself," he writes in *Mr. Sammler's Planet*. With all the comedy in his books, Bellow has a tragic view of life. His short masterpiece, *Seize the Day*, is typical with its miserly, unfeeling father, the son who craves one word of compassion from him now that his life lies in ruins, and the equally indifferent wife he is separated from. As always, Bellow strives to give each character a fair hearing. "In art you become familiar with due process," he writes in *Ravelstein*. "You can't simply write people off or send them to hell."

What makes Bellow's vision so powerful, and here I have to disagree again with his biographer, who accuses him of failing to empathize with others, is that he does. It is true that he's tough on women, but even there, it's not fair to accuse him of turning them into caricatures. Their failings are human in the eyes of the author. There's rarely an element of compassion missing from portrayals of even the most offensive characters in the novels. There's no doubting the affection in much of what he writes about children and old people. If one accepts what Atlas maintains, one might also have to conclude that a heartless bastard can write a great book.

Compassion is all-important to Bellow's vision, because without it his loners would be stuck with their solipsism. "A man is only as good as what he loves," one of his characters recollects someone saying. There's a mystical side to compassion; it's part of the quest for the essential self, a search for a truth that lies in the depths of all our beings. In his Nobel Lecture, Bellow quotes Joseph Conrad, who speaks of that "subtle but invincible conviction of solidarity that knits together the loneliness of innumerable hearts . . . which binds together all humanity—the dead to the living and the living to the unborn." Literature's highest task is to try to accomplish that. Its finest pages, Bellow thinks, can lead one into what he calls "sacred states of the soul." Anyone who has been deeply moved by a novel or a short story of his would have to agree that such an experience is, indeed, possible.

Tragi-Comic Soup: On John Ashbery

Depending on what critic one happens to read, either John Ashbery is our finest, most innovative poet of the last thirty years or he is simply just another shameless purveyor of incomprehensible, self-indulgent nonsense. There's no doubt that he is as influential today as Eliot or Lowell were in their day. In my own case, reading him over these many years, I must have learned a thing or two along the way.

Ashbery, as with any prolific poet, is occasionally bad, often exasperating, and almost always interesting. He has great poetic skills and is capable of writing a truly magnificent poem. In his twenty books of poetry, there is a body of work as original and beautiful as anyone has written in the last fifty years. Grouped with the so-called New York School of poets, who with the members of several other poetic movements in the 1950s saw themselves as subverting the conventions of the times, he has long since transcended any such label. In fact, it seems to me, the heart of Ashbery's aesthetic project is a lifelong effort to elude categories. Both the critics who conscript him as a postmodernist and claim they understand his every verbal conjuring act as well as the ones who find his poems hopelessly obscure and unreadable are wide off the mark. His poetry is far too varied and intellectually complex to permit itself to be pigeonholed. Readers of diverse tastes easily make anthologies of their Ashbery favorites, rarely duplicating a poem.

When asked about their poetic influences, poets are rarely forthright. They beat around the bush not because they're in the throes of some version of Harold Bloom's Oedipal struggle

Review of *Your Name Here* and *Other Traditions,* by John Ashbery. From the *New York Review of Books,* November 30, 2000.

with a poetic ancestor which they desperately wish to conceal, but because they truly do not know for sure. In an age when American poets are read in Siberia and French poets in Kansas, a poetic style is a concoction of many recipes from many different cuisines, so that even the most experienced epicure of verse is often hard put to identify all the ingredients that went into it. On the opening page of *Other Traditions,* a collection of his Charles Eliot Norton Lectures at Harvard, pondering why he was invited to give these talks, Ashbery speculates that the reason may be that since he is known as a writer of hermetic poetry, they most likely expect him to "spill the beans" in the course of the lectures and reveal how he does it.

Of course, a poet as hospitable as he is to a variety of poetic strategies, someone who can easily move within a single poem from high seriousness to downright silliness, echoing in the process several earlier styles of poetry and still sounding like himself, is extraordinarily difficult to pin down. He readily admits the importance of Wallace Stevens, Marianne Moore, Gertrude Stein, Elizabeth Bishop, and more surprisingly William Carlos Williams, Boris Pasternak, and Osip Mandelstam. In addition to these, he speaks in the lectures about a smaller group of poets whom he reads to get a jump-start when his batteries have run down and he needs to be reminded again what poetry is. They are all minor figures and include known names like John Clare, Laura Riding, and the French poet-novelist Raymond Roussel, little-known ones like Thomas Lovell Beddoes and John Wheelwright, and a complete unknown, David Schubert.[1] Ashbery explains:

As I look back on the writers I have learned from, it seems that the majority, for reasons I am not quite sure of, are what the world calls minor ones. Is it inherent sympathy for the underdog, which one so often feels oneself to be when one embarks on the risky business of writing? Is it desire for one-upmanship, the urge to parade one's esoteric discoveries before others? Or is there something inherently stimulating in the poetry called "minor," something it can do for us when major poetry can merely wring its hands? And what exactly is minor poetry?

No matter how its secondary status is defined, whether it is due to bad luck on the poet's part or simply a lack of merit, the strength of minor poetry, Ashbery would say, lies precisely in its imperfection. The Norton Lectures attempt to solve that puzzle, namely, the degree to which originality is the product of a peculiar kind of inability. These poets, one thinks, are like the so-called primitive painters whose vision charms us despite their lack of ability—except not really. The poets Ashbery discusses had plenty of poetic skill, so the answer must lie somewhere else. It may be that for various reasons they were incapable of obeying what were regarded as good literary manners in their day. Clare, for instance, rankled his would-be editors with radical sentiments about the plight of the rural poor and his anticlericalism. Beddoes hoped to discover the exact location of the soul through anatomical research. Wheelwright wrote by first gazing at the ocean for several days, until phrases formed themselves in his mind and he was compelled to write them down.

Our literature is full of misfits, so it is only natural that an American poet would seek them out. It takes a certain type of reader, however, to recognize them and appreciate them, a reader with a knowledge of modern poetry's experimental tradition, where poems that consist of nothing but images and fragments are common, as with Clare's "The Elm and the Ashes":

> The elm tree's heavy foliage meets the eye
> Propt in dark masses on the evening sky.
> The lighter ash but half obstructs the view,
> Leaving grey openings where the light looks through.

Or this from Beddoes:

> Like the red outline of beginning Adam.

Other Traditions is an entertaining and shrewd little book. To begin with, the life stories of the six poets he discusses are all amazing. Ashbery is an accomplished raconteur, and the lectures are full of delightful anecdotes. We learn, for instance, that Raymond Roussel wrote in the morning and only then sat down to a meal, which consisted of breakfast, lunch, and dinner

and which lasted from early to late afternoon and often con-
sisted of twenty-seven courses. His favorite dish, by the way, was
chocolate soup. The other delectations of the book are the re-
markable poems and fragments he has rescued from oblivion.
There's the astonishing David Schubert, whom he says he values
more than Pound or Eliot, and the equally gifted John Wheel-
wright, who wrote this moving poem, which I feel I must quote
in full:

Train Ride
For Horace Gregory

After rain, through afterglow, the unfolding fan
of railway landscape sidled on the pivot
of a larger arc into the green of evening;
I remembered that noon I saw a gradual bud
still white; though dead in its warm bloom;
always the enemy is the foe at home.
And I wondered what surgery could recover
our lost, long stride of indolence and leisure
which is labor in reverse; what physic recall the smile
not of lips, but of eyes as of the sea bemused.
We, when we disperse from common sleep to several
tasks, we gather to despair; we, who assembled
once for hopes from common toil to dreams
or sickish and hurting or triumphal rapture;
always our enemy is our foe at home.
We, deafened with far scattered city rattles
to the hubbub of forest birds (never having
"had time" to grieve or to hear through vivid sleep
the sea knock on its cracked and hollow stones)
so that the stars, almost, and birds comply,
and the garden-wet; the trees retire; We are
a scared patrol, fearing the guns behind;
always the enemy is the foe at home.
What wonder that we fear our own eyes' look
and fidget to be at home alone, and pitifully
put of age by some change in brushing the hair
and stumble to our ends like smothered runners at their
    tape;
We follow our shreds of fame into an ambush.
Then (as while the stars herd to the great trough

the blind, in the always-only-outward of their dismantled
archways, awake at the smell of warmed stone
or the sound of reeds, lifting from the dim
into the segment of green dawn) always
our enemy is our foe at home, more
certainly than through spoken words or from grief-
twisted writing on paper, unblotted by tears
the thought came:
There is no physic
for the world's ill, nor surgery; it must
(hot smell of tar on wet salt air)
burn in fever forever, an incense pierced
with arrows, whose name is Love and another name
Rebellion (the twinge, the gulf, split seconds,
the very raindrops, render, and instancy of Love).
All Poetry to this not-to-be-looked-upon sun
of Passion is the moon's cupped light; all
Politics to this moon, a moon's reflected
cupped light, like the moon of Rome, after
the deep well of Grecian light sank low;
always the enemy is the foe at home.
But these three are friends whose arms twine
without words; as, in still air,
the great grove leans to wind, past and to come.

There's nothing comparable in American poetry—and that's
the point Ashbery is making in his lectures. Minor poets come
to the feast of the muses, as Edmund Gosse said of Thomas
Lovell Beddoes, "bearing little except one small savory dish,
some cold preparation, we may say, of olives and anchovies, the
strangeness of which has to make up for its lack of importance."
Nonetheless, there are more than hors d'oeuvres in these talks.
Personally, I'd make Wheelwright's poem one of the entrees at
a banquet to which the most fastidious writers were invited.

The lectures also provide abundant hints about Ashbery's
own method. As he readily admits, poets when writing about
other poets frequently write about themselves. He also quotes
John Barth to the effect that writers really don't know why they
do what they do, and when they try to explain it, they talk rub-
bish. This may be true in a lot of cases, but it does not apply to
Ashbery. Anyone who is familiar with his writings on art knows

what a keen critical mind he has. Some suggestive bits from *Other Traditions* provide, along with many other similar ones in the book, an excellent description of what reading an Ashbery poem feels like:

> He begins anywhere and stops anywhere.

> Yet their shifts of tone can be . . . bewildering.

> Unlike Wordsworth's exalted rambles in "The Prelude," there is no indication that all this is leading up to something, that the result will be an enriching vision, a placing of man in harmonious relation to his God-created surroundings.

> . . . inspired *bricolage* . . .

> She made her poetry a record of her mind becoming aware of itself.

> What we are left with is a bouquet of many layered, splintered meanings, to be clasped but never fully understood.

Here is a poem from *Your Name Here* that has some of the characteristics listed above:

Bloodfits

As inevitable as a barking dog, second-hand music
drifts down five flights of stairs and out into the street,
adjusting seams, checking makeup in pocket mirror.

Inside the camera obscura, jovial as ever,
dentists make all the money. I didn't know that then.
Children came out to tell me, in measured tones,
how cheap the seaside is, how the salt air reddens cheeks.

Violently dented by storms, the new silhouettes
last only a few washings.
Put your glasses on and read the label. Hold that bat.
He'd sooner break rank than wind.
He's bought himself a shirt the color of Sam Rayburn Lake,
muddled ocher by stumps and land practices. Picnicking
    prisoners

never fail to enjoy the musk that drifts off it
in ever-thickening waves,
triggering bloody nostalgia
for a hypotenuse that never was.

The title is suggestive, but doesn't tell me anything specific. I find myself on the stairs of an apartment building with music from a radio or a record player floating down five flights like a woman all dressed up to go on a hot date. Nice image, I think. Next come the cheerful, money-grabbing dentists, and the logic of the image eludes me. What is it about a dentist's office that is like that forerunner of the photographic camera with its tiny opening through which the light passes? I'm making the assumption that the dentists are in the same building, because like most readers I take everything I'm told in a poem literally first. In other words, I need a firm foothold, and Ashbery won't let me have one. He's quick on his feet. All points of view are temporary to him. He seems to be everywhere and nowhere in his poems. Scenes, tenses, pronouns shift without the slightest warning. I suppose, instead of worrying where I am, I ought to have followed that young woman out into the street. If there are kids offering travel tips on the sidewalk, so be it.

The same goes for the new silhouettes (new identities?) that come with laundry labels and last only a few washings. Have the children been playing stickball on the street? This fellow who wears a shirt the color of a lake in Texas named after the distinguished speaker of the House of Representatives, is he asking me to join the game? At this point, the reader either gives up on the poem or figures, what the hell, let's go for a ride with it. A chain gang of prisoners straight out of a 1930s movie has just sat down for a picnic lunch at the lakeside, making someone nostalgic for the days when tough guys thought they knew all the angles, even the ones that were never there.

Ashbery can rarely write down anything without being reminded of something else. Perhaps "write" is not the correct word for how he composes. It's hard to imagine him writing the first stanza of this poem and then proceeding to the next one and the next one by a series of associations. These unexpected and mystifying shifts and gaps are to be found everywhere in his poetry, but how are they actually accomplished? Are they a meticulous transcript of his mind's ongoing activity? To me, the poems frequently feel as if they were the products of chance operations. Words and phrases found anywhere are moved around until they begin to cohere. I can imagine him getting up in the middle of a poem, reaching for any book on his shelf, opening it anywhere, or picking up the newspaper from the floor and incorporating the newly found language. He has a knack for making these fragments flow together as if they were a part of someone's interior conversation. Even more amazingly, he manages in poem after poem to make that voice intimate and distinctive.

Whatever an Ashbery poem eventually turns out to be about is not an idea he started with but something he stumbled upon as he shuffled phrases and images like a pack of cards. It's precisely because he has nothing to say initially that he is able to say something new. Poets who think they have new things to say run out of ideas quickly and are condemned to say the same thing over and over again in their poems. This may not make very much sense, but that's how it works in practice.

There's something else too. Most poets trim their experiences down to their manageable parts. If they are writing about what happened in the woods one snowy night, they are not likely to include stray thoughts they are having at that moment about taking a pair of pants to the cleaners. Ashbery does. He includes such extraneous material, no matter how irrelevant it seems to be. It is his refusal to make a choice between what is "serious" and what is "trivial" that drives his detractors batty. They want poems to tidy up experience, while he keeps insisting that messiness is part of the picture. What it comes down to is a quarrel about truth and beauty. Can a poem bear the mention of barbecued pork ribs dripping with grease and still be a lyric poem? If one believes that randomness and nonsense are an integral part of the human experience, as all comic writers always have, then those for whom poetry is synonymous with delicacy of feeling and verbal decorum will go away unhappy and even angry.

Ashbery's comic outlook goes against the grain of much of our poetry. "We live in an old soup of the tragi-comic," he says in a poem in *Your Name Here*. By taking lightly the whole idea of one meaning, he blasphemes against our transcendentalist tradition, which all but obligates the American poet to end each poem with a wholesome insight, if not a cosmic vision. "Please don't tell me if it all adds up in the end. / I'm sick of that one," he says. Most of the time he resists the temptation, although he is more than capable of composing a poem of ideas with an intricate argument and an unambiguous conclusion. Nevertheless, Ashbery is rightly wary of the way poets, as a matter of habit, contrive to sum it all up for the reader. What's the point in reading a poem, many will say, if there's no point to it? For the same reason, I would answer, that it's pleasant and even poetic to take a walk in a strange city with no destination in mind and end up getting lost.

When Whitman claimed that he contained multitudes, he was not just bragging. To a greater or lesser extent, all Americans do. There's no poet since Whitman who has had a larger vocabulary than Ashbery. Like Marcel Duchamp with his readymades, he is confident that poetry can be made of any verbal material, no matter how lowly it may be. Where he differs from the author of "Song of Myself" is that he is not interested in cataloging American reality, but in taking inventory of its various lingoes. A poem for Ashbery is a stage in a comedy club. Like a good impersonator, he's able to assume many different voices and act out the roles that go with them. There's no inflated ego in Ashbery, no belief in the firmness of the individual self. In his poems, unknown speakers address other unknown speakers or they talk to themselves as we eavesdrop. He told an interviewer in 1978, the year his *Three Plays* was published: "Perhaps I am able to write more easily when I imagine what another person might be thinking or saying. I think in my poetry one can become aware of a number of different voices carrying on a dialogue or conversation in the poem even though it's not indicated, of course, as it is in a play."[2]

Ashbery's new book of poems is one of his better ones. Once again, the many kinds of language in use today are on display: "A talent for self-realization / will get you only as far as the va-

cant lot / next to the lumber yard," is how a poem called "Life
Is a Dream" begins. Another poem in *Your Name Here* conflates
the histories of Admiral George Dewey, philosopher John
Dewey, and Melvil Dewey, the educator and innovator in library
science:

Memories of Imperialism

Dewey took Manila
and soon after invented the decimal system
that keeps libraries from collapsing even unto this day.
A lot of mothers immediately
started naming their male
offspring "Dewey,"
which made him queasy. He was already having second
    thoughts about imperialism.
In his dreams he saw library books with milky numbers
on their spines floating in Manila Bay.
Soon even words like "vanilla" or "mantilla" would cause
    him to vomit.
The sight of a manila envelope precipitated him
into his study, where all day, with the blinds drawn,
he would press fingers against temples, muttering "What
    have I done?"
all the while. Then, gradually, he began feeling a bit better.
The world hadn't ended. He'd go for walks in his old
    neighborhood,
marveling at the changes there, or at the lack of them. "If
    one is
to go down in history, it is better to do so for two things
rather than one," he would stammer, none too meaning-
    fully.

One day his wife took him aside
in her boudoir, pulling the black lace mantilla from her
    head
and across her bare breasts until his head was entangled in
    it.
"Honey, what am I supposed to say?" "Say nothing, you big
    boob.
Just be glad you got away with it and are famous." "Speaking
    of

boobs . . ." "Now you're getting the idea. Go file those
    books
on those shelves over there. Come back only when you're
    finished."

To this day schoolchildren wonder about his latter career
as a happy pedant, always nice with children, thoughtful
toward their parents. He wore a gray ceramic suit
walking his dog, a "bouledogue," he would point out.
People would peer at him from behind shutters, watchfully,
hoping no new calamities would break out, or indeed
that nothing more would happen, ever, that history had
    ended.
Yet it hadn't, as the admiral himself
would have been the first to acknowledge.

In Ashbery's poem-theater lately the repertoire consists mostly
of tragic farces. "It seems we were so happy once, just for a
minute," he says in one poem. "The failure to see God is not a
problem / God has a problem with," is how another one begins.
Ashbery is an inveterate skeptic who, like Stevens and Frost, ad-
mits only temporary stays against confusion. For him each mo-
ment of our lives, each thing we say, is equally true and false. It is
true because at the very moment we are saying it that is the only
reality, and it is false because in the next moment another reality
will replace it. Despite the insouciant tone of his poetry, Ashbery
doesn't take in stride the philosophical muddle we find ourselves
in. He knows that there's a tragic side to this farce we all play so
well, and perhaps he is never more explicit about that than in
Your Name Here. An air of deep melancholy pervades a number of
the poems so that the love poems often read like elegies. He cites
with approval in *Other Traditions* a definition of poetry from one
of David Schubert's poems:

> Speaking of what cannot be said
> To the person I want to say it.

Of course. The impossibility of ever adequately describing the
feel of time passing, the light falling in a certain way, all the
fleeting and ineffable moments that make up an individual life,

are the reasons lyric poetry has been written for over two thousand years. Ashbery, our poet with the finest ear for language, speaks of what eludes words, what lies outside them and stubbornly continues being something else:

Of the Light

That watery light, so undervalued
except when evaluated, which never happens
much, perhaps even not at all—
I intend to conserve it
somehow, in a book, in a dish, even at night,
like an insect in a light bulb.

Yes, day may just be breaking. The importance isn't there
but in beautiful flights of the trees
accepting their own flaccid destiny,
or the tightrope of seasons.
We get scared when we look at them up close
but the king doesn't mind. He has the tides to worry about,

and how fitting is the new mood of contentment
and how long it will wear thin.

I looked forward to seeing you so much
I have dragged the king from his lair: There,
take that, you old wizard. Wizard enough, he replies,
but this isn't going to save us from the light
of breakfast, or mend the hole in your stocking.
"Now wait"—and yet another day has consumed itself,
brisk with passion and grief, crisp as an illustration in a
    magazine
from the thirties, where we and this light were all that
    mattered.

"Most reckless things are beautiful in some way, and recklessness is what makes experimental art beautiful, just as religions are beautiful because of the strong possibility that they are founded on nothing," Ashbery has written.[3] Reading this book of lectures and collection of poems, we can only be grateful that he has never fooled himself for a minute into thinking that he knows now how it's done and that there's no longer any room or need for surprises.

NOTES

1. The section on Schubert was published in the *New York Review,* October 5, 2000.

2. "Interview: John Ashbery, Pact in the Theatre," *PAJ* 3, no. 3 (winter 1979), p. 16.

3. John Ashbery, *Reported Sightings: Art Chronicles, 1957–1987* (New York: Knopf, 1989), p. 391.

Stargazing in the Cinema:
On Joseph Cornell

Joseph Cornell, who died in 1972, has turned out to be one of the most admired American artists of the last fifty years. While he was certainly known in the New York art world by the late 1940s, and his name and an occasional reproduction of his work may have been seen in a book devoted to Surrealist art, his fame and wealth never approached that of a great many of his contemporaries. The boxes now on display in this country's biggest museums could still be bought for as little as $250 in the early 1950s.

In the last decade, however, the proliferation of books and essays about him has produced a vast bibliography that equals and most often surpasses those on other artists of his generation. In addition to numerous introductions to museum and gallery exhibition catalogs, a new biography, three book-length monographs, as well as a selection from his diaries, letters, and files have been published. What is striking about almost everything written about Cornell is that it tends to be unusually fine. He seems to bring out the best in art historians and critics, as this study of his "cinematic imagination" by Jodi Hauptman confirms. Cornell went about making art in such a novel way while employing such unlikely materials that making sense of what he did requires some of the originality and the imagination that went into his art.

Cornell, who could neither paint, draw, sculpt, nor hold a movie camera, is famous above all for his small, glass-fronted

Review of *Joseph Cornell: Stargazing in the Cinema,* by Jodi Hauptman. From the *New York Review of Books,* April 27, 2000.

shadow boxes with their puzzling assemblages of found objects, and less so for his collages and short films. In addition to hundreds of works of art, he left behind a vast archive of files, memorabilia, and source material on his various projects, all stored now at the Smithsonian, which the authors of these recent studies have gone over for clues. As Deborah Solomon writes in her recent biography: "It is often said of artists that they live in fear of being misunderstood. Cornell, by contrast, lived in fear of being understood."[1] Like Edgar Allan Poe and Emily Dickinson before him, Cornell was a lover of secrets and mysteries. He himself described his boxes as being like forgotten games, the abandoned games of a childhood rich in ambiguities. The art world being what it is today, Cornell's independence of mind appears worthy of emulation.

"A gourmet art by a man who ate junk food" is how Robert Motherwell described his work. Even to people who saw him fairly often he was a complete enigma. They remember him as drab looking, always preoccupied, speaking in monologues, oblivious to other people, an eccentric and a loner. Unmarried and with no sexual experience till the very last years of his life, he lived with his mother and an invalid brother who suffered from cerebral palsy in a small house on Utopia Parkway in Queens, whose basement he had turned into his studio. He ate little, never touched alcohol or set foot in the famous bars the painters and writers then frequented. He made appearances at art shows and gallery openings, greeting acquaintances and making a speedy departure. Cornell, who roamed the streets of Manhattan for almost fifty years, was usually to be found at home in Queens by eight o'clock in the evening. Except for time spent at boarding school in Massachusetts, this strange man never traveled beyond the five boroughs and their environs.

Joseph Cornell was born in Nyack on the Hudson River on December 24, 1903, a descendant of some of the oldest New York Dutch families. His father was employed for many years in woolen manufacturing, starting as a salesman and advancing to the position of a textile designer. By all accounts, he was a cheerful man in love with theater, music, and with a taste for the good life. Cornell's mother was an avid reader who even wrote a movie scenario in her youth. They had four children, of whom Joseph was the oldest. In 1917 the family's luck suddenly changed. The father died of leukemia and left them with large debts. Mrs. Cornell tried to make ends meet, baking cakes and knitting sweaters, but for many years afterward, the family struggled, living one step above poverty. Nonetheless, with the help of her husband's former boss, Cornell's mother succeeded in sending her son to Phillips Academy at Andover for four years.

Joseph was a poor student. He took courses in French language and literature and for one year was most likely a classmate of Walker Evans, another inveterate collector of images. However, he failed to fulfill the course requirements and left school without receiving a diploma. Back in New York, he went to work immediately in order to help the family, now living in Bayside, Queens. Through his father's old connections in the trade, he got work as a salesman for a textile company with offices on Madison Square. From 1921 to 1931, he made the rounds from one manufacturer to another offering his samples. Killing time between appointments, Cornell browsed in used book stores along Fourth Avenue between Union Square and the Bowery and in hundreds of junk shops from Fourteenth Street to Times Square. These were the places where the contents of many attics and immigrant suitcases ended up. One could discover just about anything on their dim shelves and in their dusty bins, something valuable or nearly worthless brought to America as a souvenir or an heirloom from St. Petersburg, Paris, Shanghai, or any other place on the face of the earth.

Long before he started making his boxes, Cornell was already a connoisseur of ephemera, bringing home to Queens old books, movie magazines, silent-film postcards, nineteenth-century toys, engravings, theatrical memorabilia, dolls, maps, and much else that anyone else would regard as nothing but trash. It's rare to encounter a young scavenger, but that's what he certainly was, obsessive and with no idea what he was going to do with his hoard. The inventory of one of his early boxes gives the idea:

Object. 1941. Box construction with velvet-paneled exterior sides, brass-ring grip, and paint-spattered glass front. Contains 3 paper parrot silhouettes, mounted on wood backings, paper cutout of 2 parakeets, corks, miniature fork and spoon, pine cone and bark, and dried leaf fronds. Back and sides of interior covered with collage of German book fragments, baby photo, paper clock face, etc. Column at left covered with collage of German book fragments with penny candy embedded in it.[2]

In November of 1931, after seeing a show of Surrealist art at the Julien Levy Gallery, he was so intrigued by some Max Ernst collages made with nineteenth-century engraved illustrations that, supposedly, he went home to Utopia Parkway and late that night, after his mother and brother had gone to sleep, made his first black-and-white collages on the kitchen table out of the old books and prints he had previously collected. One Saturday afternoon soon after, he stopped by the gallery and showed Levy three small collages he had done. Levy's surprised reaction was that these were works of Ernst he might have misplaced—or so he claims in his memoirs. Regardless of whatever truly happened that day, Cornell returned to the gallery promptly with some boxes—not the shadow boxes he's famous for and which he would not begin making till five years later, but round pillboxes he had bought in a drugstore and emptied. Cornell replaced their original contents with tiny shells, sequins, rhinestones, beads, ground red glass, black thread, and scraps of blue paper, while often retaining the original label of the product. SURE CURE FOR THAT TIRED FEELING, one of them announces. The result of this frenzied creative activity was that Levy, that same winter, not only decided to include some of Cornell's work in a new Surrealist exhibition at his gallery, but also asked him to design the cover for the catalog. These works in the show, for want of a better name, were simply called *Surrealist Toys*.

Despite the continual association of Cornell with the Surrealists, and the influence of Ernst and Duchamp on his work, which he readily acknowledged, it would be wrong to regard him as one. Mary Baker Eddy rather than André Breton was his true spiritual guide. He had converted to Christian Science at the age of twenty-three and remained a devoted practitioner all his life, making daily visits to its reading rooms and pondering its theology. There was too much black magic in Surrealism, he said. The movement's hatred of religion, explicit sexuality, black humor, and admiration for Freud and Marx were anathema to him. He was the "authentic Romantic soul," Dore Ashton aptly noted.[3] Nostalgia for happier times and for purer lost loves was still congenial to him; so was the accompanying outpouring of sentimentality, on which the Surrealists, like the rest of the Modernists, gagged. What makes Cornell so interesting and makes him difficult to categorize as an artist is that he is a tangle of antithetical aesthetic positions. Whatever the case may be, the discovery of the collage technique gave him an unexpected opportunity to "objectify" whatever impulse lay hidden behind his maniacal collecting. It also provided him with a poetics an urban wanderer such as himself could put immediately to use. Both Baudelaire and Emerson believed in the mystic religion of universal analogy, but while they sought its manifestations in nature, Cornell found his "forest of symbols" in the city. Somewhere on the island of Manhattan, there were, he believed, a few objects, dispersed in unknown locations, that rightly belonged together despite being seemingly incompatible in appearance. Starting with paper collages and eventually making them three-dimensional with the help of various kinds of boxes, Cornell gradually left behind his early influences and struck out on his own. It is worth pointing out that Cornell worked in the absence of any previous idea of beauty. A kind of flea-market democracy is present in his work. "The question is not what you look at, but what you see," Thoreau wrote somewhere in his journals. There was no separation in Cornell's mind between high and low culture. Is there another serious artist who loved both Vermeer and Barbie dolls? He shuffled trinkets within his boxes for months and years on end until he found an image that pleased him, without previous knowledge about what that image would turn out to be.

"Joseph's mind worked by association and by passionate identification with specific things, and a very acute feeling of connection between specific things, but I don't think by intellectual theory," Donald Windham wrote.[4] Fetishism far more than Surrealism is the hidden logic that brings together a threaded needle, a doll's forearm, a mirror fragment, a plastic lobster, a thimble, a yellow bead, and a dollhouse knife. Cornell saved mementos of the places and people he met while roaming the city. He writes repeatedly in his diaries of "intangible visitations," "little coincidences," "sublime moments," and of objects found shortly after such encounters that helped him preserve their memory.

A box, in that sense, is a place where the inner and the outer realities meet on a small stage. What gives the viewer an additional delight are the titles of the pieces themselves: *Soap Bubble Set, L'Egypte de Mlle Cléo de Mérode, Pharmacy, Museum, Taglioni's Jewel Casket, Hôtel du Nord, The Life of King Ludwig of Bavaria,* and more intriguingly *Penny Arcade Portrait of Lauren Bacall.* There may not be any obvious connection between the artwork and the label, but our imagination before long finds one. The boxes actually make me think of poems at their most hermetic. To engage imaginatively with one of them is like contemplating the maze of metaphors on some Symbolist poet's chessboard. The ideal box is like an unsolvable chess problem in which only a few figures remain after a long intricate game whose solution now seems both within the next move or two and forever beyond reach.

The years between 1932 and 1945 were a period of wide-ranging and hectic activity for Cornell. In addition to experimenting with different types of boxes and collages, he freelanced as a designer for *Vogue, House and Garden,* and *Dance Index.* The editors of these magazines knew of his vast image library and went to him when they needed movie and theater memorabilia. As his father did before him, he stopped being a salesman, and after a brief period of selling refrigerators door-to-door, he was hired as a designer by a textile studio. Most important, he met Marcel Duchamp, who became a lifelong friend and a booster. Cornell had his first one-man exhibition at the Julien Levy Gallery in 1932 and continued to show there and elsewhere repeatedly, in the company of the Surrealists, for the rest of the decade. He wrote a film script in 1933, *Monsieur Phot,* a movie not intended to be made but only imagined, and created his first collage movie in 1936.

Cornell's *Rose Hobart* is an example of what he called "tapestry in action." It was pieced together by cutting up found footage of a sixteen-millimeter print of an early talkie, *East of*

Borneo. Using scissors and tape, he cut the film into segments, which he then spliced out of sequence. What was originally a seventy-seven-minute feature became after Cornell's editing a plotless nineteen-minute film devoted solely to its actress. The original movie is a hackneyed jungle drama about a certain Linda, played by an actress named Rose Hobart, who travels to the ends of the earth, the fictional principality of Maradu in Indonesia, to find and bring home her drunken husband, who is a court physician to the Sorbonne-educated and dapper reigning prince. Linda resists the attempts at seduction by the spooky monarch, whose fate, it turns out, is mysteriously tied to the island's active volcano. In the movie's final scene, Linda shoots the prince as he opens the curtain to reveal the erupting volcano, and the husband-doctor, realizing the great love his wife bears him, miraculously recovers his sanity that very moment.

As Hauptman describes it in her book:

> Rose Hobart's performance in *East of Borneo* consists of anxious and twitchy movements of the body and rapidly changing facial expressions. In collating frames of the actress, Cornell seeks not to smooth out her jarring behavior but to emphasize her frenetic actions through disjunctive editing. Reveling in these joints, breaks, and splices (each of which presents another face of the actress), the artist constructs *Rose Hobart* of mismatches, awkward juxtapositions, and temporal discontinuities.

The entire effect, despite claims for the film as a work of genius by avant-garde filmmakers, strikes me as uninspired. Cornell lacks the feel for suspense or for comic timing of someone like Buster Keaton, who used montage years before him in the silent film *Sherlock, Jr.* Of course, in his own mind, Cornell imagined he was purifying the original film, rescuing and immortalizing the beauty of Hobart. It doesn't work for me. The sure touch and the impeccable aesthetic discernment of his boxes and collages are missing, not just from this movie but from all his films.

The premiere of the film took place at Levy's gallery in December of 1936 shortly after the opening of the MOMA exhibition "Fantastic Art, Dada, Surrealism." Salvador Dalí was in the audience with several other European artists when Cornell projected the film through a piece of tinted blue glass, while slowing the speed down to that of a silent movie—about two-thirds the pace of the original talkie. In place of the original sound track, he played a scratchy record with a bouncy Brazilian beat that he had picked up in a junk shop. Halfway through the film, Dalí jumped out of his chair, lunged for Cornell's throat, and had to be restrained. He went on shrieking that Cornell had stolen the idea for the film right out of his head. The cinema collage was undoubtedly an idea Dali had been mulling over and already toying with in *Un Chien Andalou* and *L'Age d'Or,* the Surrealist films he had made with Luis Buñuel a few years earlier.

Hauptman's book is a study of six of Cornell's "portrait-homages," and there's no question that she is on to something. She says, "It was Cornell's interest in motion pictures, in fact, that in many ways guided his artistic production." He kept archives on movie stars, divas, and ballet dancers both living and dead, as well as on unknown little girls (his "nymphs") whose pictures he had seen in art books and magazines. These files remind me of the ones J. Edgar Hoover kept on figures in public life. They consist of publicity photos, pictures and articles from newspapers and magazines, and his copious notes. Women obsessed this man who pretended that he had no interest in any kind of sex. We have lost sight of what poets from the days of Ovid and Catullus, and until recently, readily acknowledged. The dream of seduction, as much as anything else, is the motive for art. Poets, if truth were told, have spent more time thinking about what's under someone's skirt or inside someone's pants than about God.

Standing outside Manhattan's Hollywood Movie Theater, at Broadway and Fifty-first Street, one day in 1944, Cornell found himself hypnotized by the sight of a poster of Lauren Bacall looking out at him from behind glass and through the mist of light rain, Hauptman reports. "Memoried glances" is what he called such encounters. How to give them a second life was one of his chief aesthetic problems. Described by journalists as a combination of Marlene Dietrich, Katharine Hepburn, and Bette Davis, with overtones of Mae West and Jean Harlow, Bacall, they said, radiated as much sex as the law would allow. The movie *To Have and Have Not* (1944), costarring Humphrey Bogart, was made when she was only nineteen. Cornell saw something in her face that reminded him of his favorite stars of the silent pictures, whom he preferred to those of the present. He saw the film five or six times and started collecting material on the actress. What he was after, he explained, was not an actual scene but what one remembers from the film, more of a romantic afterglow. In that sense, *Penny Arcade Portrait of Lauren Bacall* is as much a self-portrait as it is a portrait of the actress.

The box construction he made for her, now in the Art Institute of Chicago, is worth describing in detail. It stands 20½ inches high. The interior has a Masonite panel partially stained blue. There are seven circular openings across the top covered with glass and just below them five horizontal openings containing five postcard views of the New York skyline behind blue glass panes. Below them are another five circular openings, each with parallel threads coiling around small gears. The center compartment frames the recessed black-and-white photograph of Bacall behind a blue glass pane bisected by lines of blue paint. On both sides of the center compartment, there is a single vertical compartment, each containing two columns of eight wood cubes painted blue or with a pasted-on photo of Bacall: two identical ones as a grown-up, five identical ones as a child, and four identical ones of her cocker spaniel. Beneath the central compartment are three additional small compartments, the ones on the left and right with Bacall and the middle one containing a mirror. All three are behind blue glass. A small red wood ball, when dropped from the top, travels through the labyrinthine interior by a series of hidden glass runways, past the actress's face, bringing it to life momentarily, and into the mirrored compartment across the bottom of the box before exiting through the hinged door.

Hauptman's chapter on the portrait of Bacall is both insightful and great fun. She tells of early amusement arcades in New York, with their shooting galleries, punching bags, and machines that read fortunes and tested lung capacity, and gives the history and explanation of devices called kinetoscopes and mutoscopes, which offered miniature spectacles and short narratives for the viewer: "Soon these coin-operated cabinets, filled with spools and gears that either threaded the images on celluloid in front of a light source (kinetoscope) or rapidly flipped individual cards past a peephole (mutoscope) . . . became the most popular amusement in the arcade." They were known as "Automatic Vaudeville" or "Penny Dreadfuls" and ran anywhere from sixteen to sixty seconds, ranging in subject matter from travelogues and newsreels to titles like "French High Kickers" and "Peeping Jimmie."

Lauren Bacall's portrait recalls the boundless ingenuity of these contraptions, which worked with coin, plunger, or brightly colored pinballs. "Looking into Cornell's boxes rehearses the voyeurism experienced in the cinema, and the cuts of both his collages and his visual/textual projects bear strong resemblance to filmmakers' editing strategies," Hauptman writes. Strangely, Cornell, though a filmmaker himself, preferred stills to motion pictures. The large central photograph of Bacall dominates the box and recalls the experience of a close-up in a movie. It gives the illusion of getting "close" while dramatizing both the intimacy and the unreachability of the person on the screen. "The eye of the camera," Cornell explained, is able "to ensnare the subtleties and legendary loveliness of . . . [the actress's] world." Time stops, as it were, and pure absorption takes over without the distraction of the story. What the artist wanted us to experience is Bacall's "innocence." He hoped to create a different image of her, moving away from the slinky, sultry, sexy look propagated by publicity agents to a shiny, clean look, "fumigated of Hollywood booze, cigarette smoke and slow-motion mugging." What the rest of us actually experience peeking inside this box, I would guess, is anything but that.

While Hauptman makes scattered attempts to enlist the help of psychoanalytic literature and literary theory, she is most persuasive when she follows her own hunches in unraveling the hidden verbal and visual threads of these homages. "Preserving and protecting examples of evanescent femininity," as she points out, was what drove Cornell. Nevertheless, as she herself demonstrates incidentally, works of art even when conceived out of the seamiest of motives have a way of transcending the artist's intentions. It is not easy to account for the exquisite taste and elegance of so many of his box constructions. One of his goddesses was chance. She taught him how to open himself to the unknown. He obeyed her, and he also cheated on her. Luckily, he let her lead him often enough to small, unimportant things whose beauty is as much a surprise to us as it was to him. She is the collaborator whose intimate biography it is not easy to write.

Cornell grew up with the movies, as Hauptman's book reminds us. What she says about Cornell is true of other artists as well as of poets and fiction writers. Yes, we all saw a lot of movies, but one wouldn't know it from reading most literary and art criticism. We fell in love, not just with some actor or actress, but with fleeting scenes that stayed with us for the rest of our lives. Boxed in the darkness of the movie theater, watching the projected light turn miraculously into an image on the screen, longing to be up there with the strange men and women who in that moment seem more real than our own lives—how familiar all that is. Cornell continues to be fascinating because he was able to incorporate an aspect of our experience of the modern American city rarely found in the work of other poets and artists. His one supreme insight was that the transcendental and the immutable could be found anywhere—in what is most banal, commonplace, and overlooked. Anyone who has been captivated by one of his boxes would have to agree that he was right.

NOTES

1. Deborah Solomon, *Utopia Parkway: The Life and Work of Joseph Cornell* (New York: Farrar, Straus, and Giroux, 1997), p. 336.

2. *Joseph Cornell*, ed. Kynaston McShine (New York: Museum of Modern Art, 1980), p. 289.

3. Dore Ashton, *A Joseph Cornell Album* (New York: Viking, 1974), p. 10.

4. Donald Windham, "Things That Cannot Be Said: A Reminiscence," in *Joseph Cornell Collages, 1931–1972* (Los Angeles: Corcoran Gallery, 1978), pp. 11–13.

Literature and the Gods:
Roberto Calasso

Everything, in the world, exists to end up in a book.
—Mallarmé

The surprising durability of ancient Greek myths in an age when Homer, Ovid, and other classics are no longer taught in our schools is astonishing and not easy to explain. In this country, we have never been very good at history, barely troubling to remember our own in much detail, and the same is true of the literary past, which is gradually being expunged from the curriculum. When it comes to pagan myths, most of the champions of progress take it for granted that they have nothing to say to us anymore. How wrong they are. This year, for example, saw the publication of *Gods and Mortals,* an anthology of modern poems based on classical myths.[1] Out of 323 poems in the book, roughly one-fourth are the work of contemporary American poets. When it comes to being out of sync with reigning intellectual fashions, poets get the prize every time.

As for the anthology itself, the structure is thematic, so one finds poems on almost every figure in mythology, with Orpheus and Eurydice and the wanderings and homecoming of Odysseus seeming to be the favorites. Poets who have vastly different and frequently unreconcilable ideas of poetry, such as, for example, Joseph Brodsky and Gregory Corso, Robert Creeley and Richard Wilbur, Lucille Clifton and Jorie Graham, are to be found reflecting on some god or mortal hero. To para-

Review of *Literature and the Gods,* by Roberto Calasso, trans. Tim Parks. From the *New York Review of Books,* September 20, 2001.

phrase Charles Olson, myth is a bed in which human beings continue to make love to the gods.

What is it in these stories that the poets find indispensable? The answer has to be that they still feed their imagination. What Ezra Pound said long ago still appears to be true today: "No apter metaphor having been found for certain emotional colours, I assert that gods exist." Here's a poem of his from 1912 commemorating that discovery:

The Return

See, they return; ah, see the tentative
Movements, and the slow feet,
The trouble in the pace and the uncertain
Wavering!
See, they return, one, and by one,
With fear, as half-awakened;
As if the snow should hesitate
And murmur in the wind,
     and half turn back;
These were the "Wing'd-with-Awe,"
    Inviolable,

Gods of the wingèd shoe!
With them the silver hounds,
    sniffing the trace of air!

Haie! Haie!
   These were the swift to harry;
These the keen-scented;
These were the souls of blood.

Slow on the leash,
    pallid the leash-men![2]

Even in our days of technology and globalization, it may be that the world we live in is too complex a place to explain with just one god. We need Eros, Apollo, Dionysus, Narcissus, and the rest of their tribe to make sense of things. For poets, there is also an additional motive. The big headache for over a hundred years has been how to find a larger setting for one's personal experience. Without some sort of common belief, theology, mythology—or what have you—how is one supposed to figure out what it all means? The only option remaining, or so it seems, is for each one of us to start from scratch and construct our own cosmology as we lie in bed at night. A poet who backtracks into myth is longing for a community that no longer exists. Or if it still does, it is a community of solitary readers and insomniac philosophers who are unknown to one another.

The Italian writer Roberto Calasso's book of essays *Literature and the Gods,* based on Weidenfeld Lectures he gave at Oxford, takes up this very subject of what we mean when we talk about gods. It discusses such figures as Hölderlin, Baudelaire, Nietzsche, Nabokov, Leopardi, Lautréamont, and Mallarmé and makes keen observations on several others. What is startling about Calasso's brief survey of the renewed interest in myth and pagan deities in Western literature is how recent it is in some countries. In eighteenth-century France, Greek myths were called childish fables, Shakespeare was seen as barbaric, and biblical tales were regarded as nothing more than priestly indoctrination to suffocate any potentially free spirit and enlightened mind. While the gods were never entirely lost sight of, supplying a bit of rhetorical dazzle and moral allegory in occasional poems and plays, only in painting, Calasso argues, did they run free over the centuries:

> Thanks to its wordless nature, which allows it to be immoral without coming out and saying as much, the painted image was able to restore the gods to their glamorous and terrifying apparitions as simulacra. Hence a long and uninterrupted banquet of the gods runs parallel with Western history from Botticelli and Giovanni Bellini, through Guido Reni and Bernini, Poussin and Rembrandt (*The Rape of Persephone* would itself suffice), Saraceni and Furini and Dossi, right through to Tiepolo.

With the Romantics, the world of the Greeks returns as a lost paradise and an aesthetic ideal. Speaking about gods became acceptable again. There's hardly a European poet in the nineteenth century who did not mention them. Their reasons were often superficial: they wanted to sound noble, exotic, pagan, erotic, erudite, or poetic. According to Calasso, the attraction of these antique fables for someone like Leopardi was that they were the mysterious remnants of a world where reason hadn't yet been able to unleash the full effects of its lethal power, "a power that 'renders all objects to which it turns its attention small and vile and empty, destroys the great and the beautiful and even, as it were, existence itself.'"

This attitude, as Leopardi himself realized, was absurd. Pretending to be ancient Romans or Greeks while concealing the fact that they were modern Europeans made some of the poets look silly. In France, among the Parnassians and Symbolists, that silliness had a use: it sheltered one against the vulgarity of the shopkeeper. "Everything can be at home in this century but poetry," Leopardi wrote, a sentiment far removed from what Emerson and Whitman were saying a few years later; for them, in America at least, this was the golden age for poets.

❧

"Difficult are the gods for men to see," the ancient *Hymn to Demeter* already complains. Before they became literary clichés, the pagan deities lived the quiet lives of exiles in our midst, revealing their true nature only to a select few. The more modern literature tried to be absolutely original, the more it rummaged in the unconscious, the more it came face to face with them. Once again Orpheus picked up his lute, Venus seduced mortal men, Sisyphus shouldered his rock, and Odysseus dallied with Calypso. As Calasso points out—and there's no disputing him—perhaps only to Hölderlin among the poets did the gods show themselves in their full radiance. Yet their supreme mystery has always been close. "Whatever else it might be, the divine is certainly the thing that imposes with maximum intensity the sensation of being alive," Calasso writes. Where we find ourselves fully awake, divinities make their appearance. Emily Dickinson used the word "awe" to describe that experience in which the entire familiar world loses its normal significance and leaves one speechless in the presence of something one can no longer name. For us moderns, these cannot be the same gods as of old. Calasso writes:

They are no longer made up of just the one family, however complicated, residing in their vast homes on the slopes of a single mountain. No, now they are multitudes, a teeming crowd in an endless metropolis. It hardly matters that their names are often exotic and unpronounceable, like the names one reads on the doorbells of families of immigrants. The power of their stories is still at work. Yet there is something new and unusual about the situation: this composite tribe of gods now lives *only* in its stories and scattered idols. The way of cult and ritual is barred, either because there is no longer a group of devotees who carry out the ritual gestures, or because even when someone does perform these gestures they stop short. The statues of Shiva and Vishnu still drip with offerings, but Varuna is a remote and shapeless entity to the Indian of today, while Prajapati is only to be found in books. [Varuna was the supreme lord of the cosmos, the keeper of divine order. Prajapati was the lord of creation.] And this, one might say, has become the natural condition of the gods: to appear in books—and often in books that few will ever open. Is this the prelude to extinction? Only to the superficial observer. For in the meantime all the powers of the cult of the gods have migrated into a single, immobile and solitary act: that of reading.

The effect of such solitary acts of piety and devotion of the few, as Calasso has amply shown, ought not to be underestimated. Two of his previously translated books, *The Marriage of Cadmus and Harmony* (1993) and *Ka* (1998), are formidably ambitious attempts to retell the stories of Greek and Indian mythology, untangle their many variants, and meditate on their meaning. "Stories," he writes about the Greeks, "never live alone: they are the branches of a family that we have to trace back, and forward." It is the same with India: "So many things happening, so many stories one inside the other, with every link hiding yet more stories." Calasso serves as our guide in the maze.

Both of these books have been extravagantly praised, and deservedly so. In the ambition of the undertaking and wealth of material, they are comparable to Ovid's *Metamorphoses* or *The Thousand and One Nights,* except the end result is very different.

What Calasso has done is original and difficult to classify. The stories not only reassemble the ancient myths into a new synthesis, but also include literary, philosophical, and historical commentary. Still, despite their extraordinary erudition and insight into the minds of these two cultures, these are not scholarly studies. They are powerful works of the imagination in their own right that will most likely inspire future generations of mythographers and poets.

Calasso refreshes our memory of how violent the myths are. Murder, rape, incest, and acts of unbelievable cruelty are matters of course. It is a world in which innocents suffer, justice is infrequent, and when it does come, it often comes too late. The trouble with too many poems on classical myths is that they are often no more than a pretext for lyric posturing, an evocation of the beauty of the bygone world and its ill-fated heroes and heroines at the expense of the harsher vision of the original. The perennial challenge in recounting myth, it seems to me, is how to make believable a pretty girl who is half fish and whose song mesmerizes sailors.

Calasso is a consummate storyteller, mixing drama, gossip, and even passages of poetry. He brings to life the ancient soap operas with their large cast of divine and human characters and keeps us entertained. Like all good stories and poems, the myths have many layers of meaning, which Calasso's cunningly told narratives manage to preserve. Did ideas come first and the myths come afterward in order to illustrate them, or did the Greeks discover them as they listened to the stories? Here is an example of what I have in mind, from Calasso's re-creation of the myth of Persephone, the goddess of fertility who was carried off into the underworld by Hades (Pluto). In the Eleusinian mysteries she appears under the name Kore:

> It was a place where dogs would lose their quarry's trail, so violent was the scent of the flowers. A stream cut deep through the grass of a meadow that rose at the edge to fall sheer in a rocky ravine into the very navel of Sicily. And here, near Henna, Kore was carried off. When the earth split open and Hades' chariot appeared, drawn by four horses abreast, Kore

was looking at a narcissus. She was looking at the act of look-ing. She was about to pick it. And, at that very moment, she was herself plucked away by the invisible toward the invisible.

What fascinates Calasso is that moment of heightened con-sciousness. Kore sees herself reaching for a narcissus, just as Hades snatches her away to be his bride. Interestingly, Calasso writes that her name doesn't just mean "girl" but "pupil" of the eyes. In the myth she turns away from the beautiful flower, their eyes meet, and she sees her pupil reflected in his. If, as Socrates claims, and Calasso points out, the Delphic maxim "Know Thy-self" can be understood as "Look at Thyself," this marvelous story of the double gaze conveys a magnificent insight. As our consciousness divides to observe itself—observation for which looking at a narcissus is an evident metaphor—that invisible other watching within us is no other than our death, as it were. In other words, and this strikes me as both true and astonishing, we come to our self-knowledge through the eye of our mortality since, obviously, if we were going to be around forever such ex-periences would not be so precious.

The Greeks, as Calasso demonstrates, had more in mind. For them, this moment is not just about self-knowledge but also about aesthetics. Our precarious life, fleeting and irreplaceable, has another dimension. That which exists once and only once is beautiful, the myths keep telling us. It is precisely because we are mortal beings that things have a significance and an intense presence at times. To come to understand that was a momen-tous discovery for literature. What has lyric poetry been for al-most three thousand years, one can ask, but an aesthetic justifi-cation of mortality?

"The first enemy of the aesthetic was meaning," Calasso writes in *The Marriage of Cadmus and Harmony*. In the aesthetic experience the meaning is there, but it doesn't impose itself. What dominates is a presence of someone or something one does not wish to name just then. The search for meaning takes one away from what is there before one's eyes. Once again, Calasso is calling attention to the moment of heightened con-sciousness, its self-sufficiency and the wordless understanding that comes with it. Like a "pure light of midsummer," such is the presence of the god Dionysus, according to the poet Pindar. Perfection always keeps something hidden, says Calasso. And to conceal with light was always the Greeks' specialty.

ॐ

If our own classic myths still resonate imaginatively and philosophically for us, what about the ones from India? At first reading *Ka,* one is overwhelmed by the unfamiliarity of the names, the oddness of the stories, and their endlessly metamorphosing divinities. We are likely to be baffled by the plurality of viewpoints, clashing metaphysical ideas, and the difficulty of drawing a distinction between different traditions and schools of thought. Once again, Calasso's prose, in Tim Parks's masterful translation, casts its narrative spell. Eventually one begins to situate oneself in an exotic universe. As in Greece, the enigma of consciousness—that light capable of seeing what it illuminates—is at the center of cosmic mystery, as it was understood by the Aryans (or Aryas) who invaded India around 1500 B.C.:

> Just as some claim that every true philosopher thinks but one thought, the same can be said of a civilization: from the beginning the Aryas thought, and India has ever continued to think, the thought that dazzled us *ṛṣis*: the simple fact of being conscious. There is not a shape, not an event, not an individual in its history that cannot, in a certain number of steps, be taken back to that thought, just as Yājñavlkya demonstrated that the three thousand, three hundred and six gods could all be taken back to a single word: *brahman.*

Here is an Indian myth that reads like a sequel to the Greek one about Kore and Hades:

> The Person in the Eye is not born alone, cannot exist alone. The first couple were the two Persons in the Eye. In the right eye was Death. In the left eye his companion. Or again: in the right eye was Indra [the warrior god and thunder god of the Vedas]. In the left eye his partner Indrānī. It was for these two that the gods made that division between the eyes: the nose. Behind the barrier of the nose two lovers hide, as though separated by a mountain. To meet, to touch, they must go down

together into the cavity that opens up in the heart. That is their bedroom. There they twine in coitus. Seen from outside, the eyes of the sleepers are hidden by the eyelids as though by a curtain around a bed. Meanwhile, in the heart's cavity, Indra and Indrāni are one inside the other. This is the supreme beatitude.

What is truly extraordinary, as Calasso convincingly shows in *Literature and the Gods,* is that in the guise of what he calls "absolute literature" some of the mythic Indian ideas seem to reappear in the West. He is not talking about direct influence of Indian thought or mythology, which was largely unknown in the nineteenth century, but of an authentic independent discovery by Western poets of similar perceptions. Of course, before any of that was possible, poetry had to free itself from the obligation to be socially relevant. Poets were now saying that poetry is like music, a language that cannot be paraphrased into another language. It is a knowledge that refuses to be subject to any other knowledge, in touch with the nameless origins of everything, the home of even the gods themselves.

One gets a better idea of what Calasso has in mind from his lecture on Isidore Ducasse, the nineteenth-century French poet who wrote under the name of the Comte de Lautréamont. *Les Chants de Maldoror,* that notorious work of macabre humor and hallucinatory erotic imagery, was written, as he says, "on the principle that *anything* and *everything* must be the object of sarcasm," not just the posturing of his contemporaries with their sniveling self-pity and romantic melancholy, but even those who raged against it like Baudelaire. Before he died at the age of twenty-four in 1870, Ducasse lived entirely in books. He drew all his material from them, freely stole passages from classics and rewrote them reversing their meanings. The word "*chants*" in the title makes one expect a book of songs, perhaps a French equivalent of *Song of Myself.* Instead, we find an anti-Whitman who exults in mixing up genres. As his translator Alexis Lykiard notes, in Ducasse we get prose poetry, poetic prose, the gothic fantasy, the serial novel, horror and humor, authorial interventions, disruptions of space and time, stories within stories, plagiarism, techniques of collage, changes of style as frequent as his hero Maldoror's own metamorphoses, and an elliptical rather than linear structure.

Rimbaud is undoubtedly a better poet, and his *Illuminations* and *A Season in Hell* have been far more influential works, but they lack Ducasse's poisonous air of mockery. For him, writers are stooges, and so is every literary propriety. He thought, Calasso writes, that "literature is a continuum of words to be interfered with as one pleases, by transforming every sign into its opposite, if that's what we want." Previously, even the most rebellious literature stayed in touch with some version of the real world. Ducasse got rid of all that. "Any literature that challenges the eternal truths is condemned to feed only on itself," he wrote. And he did just that.

The two finest essays in Calasso's new book are on Stephane Mallarmé. In the century of exact sciences, confident positivism in philosophy, and naturalism and realism in literature, Mallarmé cultivated obscure inner states and spoke approvingly of an art consecrated to fictions. In a piece based on a lecture given at Oxford and Cambridge Universities in 1894, he writes:

> Description conceals the fullness and intrinsic virtues of monuments, the sea and the human face; *evocation, allusion* or *suggestion,* though somewhat casual terms, point to what may be a very decisive trend in literature, one which both limits and sets free; for the special charm of the art lies not in the handful of dust, so to speak, not in the containing of any reality through description, in a book or a text, but in freeing from it the spirit, that volatile dispersion which is the musicality of nothing.[3]

Here modern literature and ancient myths meet. Without knowing the Vedic texts and with only a superficial acquaintance with Buddhism, Mallarmé was trying to give a name to a process at the heart of old esoteric traditions. It kept eluding him, but he made great poetry out of his attempt to do so. "There must be something occult in the ground of everyone," is how he described it in a letter. "I firmly believe in something hidden away, a closed and secret signifier, that inhabits the ordinary." "Yes, I *know,*" he writes in another letter, "we are nothing but vain for of matter—yet sublime too when you think that we invented God and our own souls." About Mallarmé, Calasso writes that never had poetry been so magnificently superimposed upon the most mysterious and elementary fact of all, the very medium in which every quality and every likeness appear, and which is called consciousness. What draws him to Mallarmé is the poet's recognition of that truth, which Calasso himself has chased after in all his books. For Mallarmé and Calasso, as for Heidegger, thinking of Being is the only way to deal with poetry.[4] In their different ways they also have a longing for the absolute and are ready to go for broke. For them, the game of being and nothingness is the supreme game, the only one worth playing.

&

"There is a very strong and very ancient emotion," Calasso writes, "that is rarely mentioned or recognized: it is the anguish we feel for the absence of idols. If the eye has no image on which to rest, if there's nothing to mediate between the mental phantasm and that which simply is, then a subtle despondency creeps in." The oldest dream ever recorded, it turns out, is told by a woman, the overseer of a palace in Mesopotamia, who in her dream enters the temple and finds that the statues have vanished and so have the people who worshiped them. For Calasso, literature is the guardian of every such space haunted by phantoms: "For whatever they may be, the gods manifest themselves above all as mental events. Yet, contrary to the modern illusion, it is the psychic powers that are fragments of the gods, not the gods that are fragments of the psychic powers." Before they could come back, literature had to find again that place, inscribed in the very ground of our being, where they have always made their presence known

Mallarmé has been both an ideal and a dead end for poets. His greatness, Octavio Paz wrote, "lies not just in his attempt to create
uld be the magic double of the universe—the
a Cosmos—but above all in the consciousness
of transforming that language into theater,
h man."[5] Once there's nothing left but a few
he initiates, what started out as a new under-
ics has turned into mysticism. A poem cannot

be pure: it is a marriage of contradictions, reverence and blasphemy, asceticism and sensuality. As much as I admire Calasso's uncompromising search for the heart of the poetic, I'm not convinced that such a search is the best way to go about writing poetry. The most attractive and puzzling aspect of the long history of poetry is that no conception of the poem is final.

Literature is never the product of a single agent, Calasso tells us. There are always at least three actors: the hand that writes, the voice that speaks, the god who watches over and compels. They could be called the I, the Self, and the Divine. The relationship between them is constantly changing as they take turns viewing themselves and the world. Mallarmé, Calasso says, gave notice that having left by society's front door, literature was back through a cosmic window, having absorbed in the meantime nothing less than everything. Calasso concludes his study by saying that we still draw sustenance from this "daring fiction." We undoubtedly do, while reminding ourselves that the search for the absolute doesn't always take place in such a rarefied atmosphere, but has to contend with everything else human beings do, from tossing and turning all night with a toothache to falling in love with someone who doesn't care whether you exist. The best critique of absolute literature is to be found in Calasso's three books on myth, where that crowning paradox is never forgotten. Besides, as he himself has told us, the gods get bored with men who have no stories to tell.

NOTES

1. *Gods and Mortals: Modern Poems on Classical Myths,* ed. Nina Kossman (New York: Oxford University Press, 2001).

2. Ezra Pound, *Selected Poems* (New York: New Directions, 1949), p. 24.

3. *Symbolism: An Anthology,* ed. and trans. T. G. West (New York: Methuen, 1980), p. 8.

4. For Calasso's reflections on Heidegger, Kafka, Flaubert, Nietzsche, Marx, Freud, Walter Benjamin, and Karl Kraus, among others, see the collection of his essays *Forty-nine Steps,* trans. John Shepley (Minneapolis: University of Minnesota Press, 1998).

5. Octavio Paz, *The Bow and the Lyre,* trans. Ruth L. C. Simms (New York: McGraw Hill, 1975).

The Strength of Poetry:
On James Fenton

If nobody reads poetry anymore, as even people who ought to know better seem to believe, who then bothers to read books about poetry? The answer is, someone obviously must since they do get published and our publishers are not known for being sentimental fools. For those skeptical of any claims made on behalf of poetry, especially of the modern variety, the probable assumption is that these books are even more obscure, even more irrelevant than the poems themselves.

Like most widespread beliefs about poetry, this one is also wrong. Not only is much contemporary verse readable and worth anybody's time, but the same can be said of some writing about poetry. This collection of lectures James Fenton delivered at Oxford demonstrates that to be the case. Notwithstanding what one thinks about Fenton's treatment of various poets under discussion, he has written a fine book, one that any general reader of literature would have absolutely no difficulty understanding and enjoying.

Fenton's writing is conspicuously free of the contemporary scholarly jargon that has made most academic writing on poetry an ordeal to read. There are no trendy terms such as "logocentricism," "signification," "slippage," "code," "textuality," "patriarchy," "hegemony," or "post-individualism" in these lectures. Academic critics, working on the premise that the issues they are dealing with are of such complexity that ordinary words simply won't do, use these concepts repeatedly to give the impression

Review of *The Strength of Poetry*, by James Fenton. From the *New York Review of Books*, July 19, 2001.

that they have reached an advanced, more radical stage of thinking about literature. At their worst, they remind me of the way literary critics in Communist Russia peppered their pieces with all-purpose catchphrases of Marx, Lenin, and Stalin even when they came to write about Homer and Shakespeare. Of course, they were obliged to do so, often at the point of a gun, and our critics are not. Nonetheless, like their Marxist counterparts, some have legitimate questions about literary works. For instance, who is the real author of a poem? Is it the poet's social class, gender, or race that writes the poem? Schools of literary criticism and the writings of poets themselves can be divided by how they answer that question.

Here are just a few possible ways:

1. The poet and no one else writes the poem.
2. The unconscious of the poet writes the poem.
3. All of past poetry writes the poem.
4. Language itself writes the poem.
5. Some higher power, angelic or demonic, writes the poem.
6. The spirit of the times writes the poem.

Probably all of these have a role in any work, but dogmatic criticism likes to pretend that there is only one correct viewpoint, be it linguistic, semantic, rhetorical, formal, structural, archetypal, or ideological. Instead of engaging the work at hand from various standpoints, it concentrates on one of these aspects of the poem to the exclusion of all the others. A critic like Fenton, who works on the assumption that any single, overall theory of poetry cannot succeed, is bound to be regarded as a relic of an earlier, unenlightened age when literary interpretation was not a science but merely the intuitive findings of an attentive reader who is not ashamed to admit that he mostly reads for pleasure.

Not surprisingly, with all its latest tools of exegesis, academic criticism has a difficult time with the lyric poem, which in most cases tends to be either unparaphrasable or completely transparent, making it difficult to erect a theoretical frame around it. In other words, it seems to resist interpretation. It won't reveal to us the secret of how it came about or how it seduces the reader. As Fenton puts it succinctly:

> There must *be* such a thing as causality, we assume; but we cannot expect to understand its workings. In the writing of poetry we may say that the thing we predict will not happen. If we can predict it, it is not poetry. We have to surprise ourselves. We have to outpace our colder calculations.

This is the crux of the problem. If there's no clear relationship between cause and effect—goodbye theory. And if there's no theory, how is the intellect going to revenge itself against the imagination by locking it up in some conceptual cage? It is worth emphasizing that the poet is not in control of his poems. He is like someone who imagines he is driving from New York to Boston only to find himself in Tuscaloosa, Alabama. The point being, we cannot turn to our imagination and say, give me an original description of what the moon looks like tonight because I need it for the poem I'm writing. An image like Rimbaud's famous "Madame X installed a piano in the Alps" literally pops out of nowhere. Our intellect wants to understand how poetry works, but it has no ability to cough up a single poetic image worth making a fuss about.

Here's a poem by Seamus Heaney that Fenton says went straight into his personal anthology:

The Butter-Print

Who carved on the butter-print's round open face
A cross-hatched head of rye, all jags and bristles?
Why should soft butter bear that sharp device
As if its breast were scored with slivered glass?

When I was small I swallowed an awn of rye.
My throat was like a standing crop probed by a scythe.
I felt the edge slide and the point stick deep
Until, when I coughed and coughed and coughed it up,

My breathing came dawn-cold, so clear and sudden
I might have been inhaling airs from heaven
Where healed and martyred Agatha stares down
At the relic knife as I stared at the awn.

Fenton's explanation of why he admires it so much will further clarify what I have in mind:

> "The pleasure and surprise of poetry," says Heaney, is "a matter of angelic potential" and "a motion of the soul." When I look at a poem like this for the first time, I ask myself: How did it do that? How did we get from the butter-print to heaven and back down to the "awn" so quickly? It's like watching the three-card trick in Oxford Street. Suddenly the table is folded up under the arm and the trickster vanishes in the crowd—excepting that, when you tap your pocket, you find you have something valuable you could have sworn wasn't there just a moment before.

How one deals with these methodological issues depends on what one believes poetry to be in the first place. Is poetry a state of mind anyone may have from time to time or a gift only a rare few are blessed with? Should our readings and interpretations of poetry follow the same ground rules as our interpretations of deeply felt experiences, or do we need experts? Is the work of a true poet an original creation that sets its own rules or the product of socially constructed reality? Does poetry take place on the deepest level of being or in that part of consciousness where our ideas and opinions are formed? Finally, is poetry more at home at the town dump or in the town library?

ও

When one writes about a poet, one's primary effort involves trying to locate some quality of the imagination or voice—that one-of-a-kind aspect—that is present regardless of whatever purpose it has been put to. Note that I say nothing of the subject matter, nor is Fenton overly concerned with it in his lectures. How he brings to light that unique quality in the poets he is discussing, I find most interesting. What he does is not unlike what a novelist strives to do in conveying the peculiarities of his or her characters. Obviously, we have to see them, hear them, and feel their singularity if they are going to make an impact on us in the story. Fenton achieves that effect in his book by a kind of collage of different approaches. He does not shy away from literary ideas and very close reading of poems, but he combines them with close scrutiny of poets' biographies in search of small, revelatory details that not only bring the individual to life but also make us recall their poems.

He loves a good anecdote. For example, he tells about Marianne Moore's father, who went mad briefly after losing his fortune in the development of the smokeless furnace, and how, when he recovered sufficiently, he got employment at the same mental institution where he had been committed. Then there's the story about Elizabeth Bishop as a college student going to hear Edna St. Vincent Millay read her poetry. On that solemn occasion, for which Millay wore a long artistic robe and clutched a curtain while she recited her poems, Bishop and her friends sat doubled up with laughter. These lady poets, she thought, were always boasting about how "nice" they were. They had to make quite sure the reader was not going to misplace them socially. Of course, that kind of anxiety interfered with what they wrote. This is what Bishop called "our beautiful old silver" school of female writing, and this little tableau of Millay tells it all.

The Strength of Poetry has chapters on Wilfred Owen, Philip Larkin, Seamus Heaney, Marianne Moore, Elizabeth Bishop, Sylvia Plath, and D. H. Lawrence, three chapters on Auden, and separate chapters on poets' vicious rivalries and on poetry that celebrates imperialism. Fenton is both a debunker and a defender of various claims made by poets. If it is true that poets do not really know how their poems come about, it is best to take both the statements they make about their work and the persona that emerges from their poetry with a grain of salt. Larkin's poems, as Fenton reminds us, seem to say:

> I detest dishonesty in writing; I detest self-mythologizing; if nothing of note happened in my childhood, I'm the kind of guy who's prepared to say so, rather than dress up non-events as events. Taken as lyric, the poem asserts its own right. It stands alone, as any lyric stands alone, to convince us, or not, on its own terms.

It sounds as if Larkin's telling the truth, but he is not. Behind his pose, there are many evasions. When he wrote in one famous poem, "They fuck you up, your mum and dad. / They may not mean to, but they do," he may have expressed something true of us all, but he got the idea at home. His father was an admirer of Hitler and even attended Nuremberg rallies. He didn't alter his views during the war and continued to praise the efficiency of Germans even during the blitzing of Coventry, where the family lived. As Fenton says, having his father call down a curse on the city must have made quite an impact on young Larkin. He also concealed his wartime rejection from military service for medical reasons. Under his air of indifference, he was a troubled man, so perhaps cause and effect do operate after all in the creative process, however sneakily? Isn't this also the case with Moore, Plath, Bishop, Auden, and so many other poets with their complicated personal histories?

ॐ

Fenton, for the most part, is an astute psychologist. He knows that there are times when biography helps unlock the poetry. Certainly, if in one's youth one's parents paraded naked around the house and chased the mailman down the block in that condition, that just may turn out to make a difference. He also knows that, luckily for poets, poems often end up having a more wholehearted vision than their authors have. Nor does he believe that there's such a thing as an artistic personality. The genius of poetry makes house calls, but he or she is not picky and may often seek out some worthless human being.

As for women poets, Fenton has this to say:

> Something held women back when it came to the writing of poetry, and since whatever it was that held them back failed to hold women back from writing novels, we must suppose that the inhibition had something, at least, to do with the antiquity and prestige of the art.

This doubtlessly is historically true. He goes on to quote Germaine Greer to the effect that it was women who deified the poet, who fainted when Byron came into the room, and states that because of that adoration they were not able to write poetry. What's missing from this account is Sappho, who did originate a type of intimate lyric that after twenty-six centuries still sounds fresh. Not only that. It is still in my view the most radical invention in all of poetry. Thanks to that kind of lyric poem, ordinary mortals make their appearance in literature for the first time. Instead of myths, with their gods and heroes larger than life, we get the first breath of realism, someone's solitary voice speaking to us directly about what concerns her at that moment.

We know the fate of Sappho's poems, how thoroughly they were censored and destroyed, first by antiquity and thereafter by the Christian zealots. They knew what she had committed was an outrage. She made the lyric self into the sacred center, if not the sacred cow, of poetry while the tribe with its beloved epics was relegated to the background. Subsequently, it was all right for a man to write like that, to be a Catullus or Propertius, but no woman could get away with it until Modernism made scandal a part of its bag of tricks.

I bring this up to amplify Fenton's point that neither Moore nor Bishop seems to have traced her ancestry back through the line of women poets. True enough. On the other hand, one can imagine Sappho understanding where many of Plath's poems were coming from. I doubt there were elms in ancient Lesbos, but this great twentieth-century poem by Plath would have sounded familiar to her.

Elm

I know the bottom, she says. I know it with my great tap root:
It is what you fear.
I do not fear it: I have been there.

Is it the sea you hear in me,
Its dissatisfactions?
Or the voice of nothing, that was your madness?

Love is a shadow.
How you lie and cry after it.
Listen: these are its hooves: it has gone off, like a horse.

All night I shall gallop thus, impetuously,
Till your head is a stone, your pillow a little turf,
Echoing, echoing.

Or shall I bring you the sound of poisons?
This rain now, this big hush.
And this is the fruit of it: tin-white, like arsenic.

I have suffered the atrocity of sunsets.
Scorched to the root
My red filaments burn and stand, a hand of wires.

Now I break up in pieces that fly about like clubs.
A wind of such violence
Will tolerate no bystanding: I must shriek.

Moore and Bishop would have been unintelligible to Sappho for numerous reasons. Fenton reminds us that every line of Moore's "went first past her mother's censorship and was later offered to her minister brother, who considered each of her poems as a spiritual event." Women unquestionably had a tradition which men helped themselves to for centuries, but from which women stayed away because their upbringing would not allow them to acknowledge something so disrespectful. Bishop herself was extremely shy. She did not like intimate sexual details spelled out and was upset when her friend Robert Lowell started confessing them in his poems. It was not gushiness but the power of reticence that she valued in a poem. Still, one suspects that occasionally she would have preferred to write more freely about personal matters, as some of the posthumously published poems show. As for Moore, who, too, was a rebel against poetic conventions, even without her mother peeking over her shoulder as she wrote, it is hard to imagine that her oddly sexless poem "Marriage" would have turned out any differently.

ॐ

The concluding three lectures in *The Strength of Poetry* deal with W. H. Auden, his writings on Shakespeare's sonnets, the influences on him of Blake and Henry James, and his peripatetic life and melancholy old age. In Fenton's account, Auden experienced firsthand the political and moral crisis of the age, the conflict between reason and heart, individual and collective, as he clung to impossible ideals, failed, turned on himself, kept his integrity, only to find himself hated and have his greatest moment of courage taken for cowardice when he remained in the United States while England was at war. At the end, in his homelessness, he comes across as a tragic figure:

> Blake sat at Auden's left when he wrote, urging concision, definite views, plain language. He was not the Blake of the long line, of the interminable prophetic books, but the fiery Blake of *The Marriage of Heaven and Hell,* the Blake of the notebooks.
> Henry James sat on Auden's right, suggesting fascinating syntaxes and ways of prolonging a sentence, giving a nuance to a nuance.

Auden needed influences, Fenton writes—and who doesn't? "We steal from our masters. We steal from our friends, from our enemies even," he says elsewhere. I would also reiterate that men steal from women and women from men. Poets have always been thieves. In the last hundred years, with the proliferation of translations, this has gotten even worse. Everybody is reading everybody else and being influenced by someone from another culture. That's why anthologies based on race and gender are suspect. Reading the poems by Auden that Fenton quotes, I was struck again by how inbred poetry is, how many echoes of our long lyrical tradition are to be found in them:

> Dear, though the night is gone,
> The dream still haunts to-day
> That brought us to a room
> Cavernous, lofty as
> A railway terminus,
> And crowded in that gloom
> Were beds, and we in one
> In a far corner lay.
>
> Our whisper woke no clocks,
> We kissed and I was glad
> At everything you did,
> Indifferent to those
> Who sat with hostile eyes
> In pairs on every bed,
> Arms round each other's necks,

Inert and vaguely sad.

What hidden worm of guilt
Or what malignant doubt
Am I the victim of,
That you then, unabashed,
Did what I never wished,
Confessed another love;
And I, submissive, felt
Unwanted and went out?

Poets seek that elusive something called poetry, and so do those who write about them. Fenton is very much aware of that in his lectures, and that is part of their strength. Paradoxically, what is most important in a poem, that *something* for which we go back to it again and again, cannot be articulated. The best one can do under the circumstances is to give the reader a hint of what one has experienced reading the poem, but is unable to name. And when that fails, one can quote the poem itself in full, because only poems can trap the "poetic"—whatever that is. Poetry's strength lies in its endless elusiveness to the intellect. This is the reason why poems continue to be written everywhere in the world and why there are still people trying to convince others that reading them will not only give pleasure but also remind the reader of poetry's strange ability to safeguard the power of our most ordinary words.

A World Gone Up in Smoke:
Czeslaw Milosz

In this world
we walk on the roof of Hell
gazing at flowers

—Issa

"They wrote as if History had little to do with them"—that's how I imagine some future study of American poetry describing the work of our poets in the waning years of the twentieth century. Like millions of their fellow citizens, they believed they could, most of the time, shut their eyes to the world, busy themselves with their lives, and not give much thought to evil. A hermetic literary culture, Czeslaw Milosz would say, is a cage in which one spends all one's time chasing one's own tail. To realize from one's own experience that there's nothing, no matter how vile, that human beings will not do to one another was until recently a knowledge reserved for the thousands of immigrants whose life stories, had they been able to make sense of them, would have still sounded farfetched and incoherent. Anyone who lived through and survived the many horrors of the last century found himself with an experience nearly incommunicable to someone who still had faith in the basic goodness of man.

Milosz spent the years between 1939 and 1945 in Warsaw, when, as he says, "Hell was spreading over the world like a drop of ink on blotting paper." That war and the years of occupation were much bloodier in Poland than in the West. In Eastern

Review of *New and Collected Poems, 1931–2001* and *To Begin Where I Am: Selected Essays,* by Czeslaw Milosz, ed. Bogdana Carpenter and Madeline G. Levine. From the *New York Review of Books,* December 20, 2001.

European countries, populated as they were by people meant to be completely exterminated or used solely for manual labor, the war killed millions and nearly destroyed the entire moral foundation of these societies. The unthinkable happened, replacing overnight what one used to regard as normal life the day before. In one of the earliest poems in *New and Collected Poems,* written in 1932, Milosz acknowledges the seemingly impossible task the poet now has before him:

> One life is not enough.
> I'd like to live twice on this sad planet,
> In lonely cities, in starved villages,
> To look at all evil, at the decay of bodies,
> And probe the laws to which the time was subject,
> Time that howled above us like a wind.

Czeslaw Milosz was born in 1911 in Szetejnije, a region of Lithuania contested after Poland became an independent state in 1918. His father was a civil engineer who served in the Imperial Russian Army in World War I, and traveled with his family all over Russia erecting bridges and fortifications behind the front lines. The young poet studied at King Stefan Batory University in Wilno (present-day Vilnius), from which he received a law degree in 1934. He published poems in a student magazine at the university, where he was also involved in leftist politics—he later said that those who had no acquaintance with Marxism would have trouble understanding its appeal. Afterward, he traveled to France on a scholarship to study literature. His first book of poetry, *A Poem on Frozen Time,* came out in 1933, followed by *Three Winters* in 1936. When Germany invaded Poland in 1939, Milosz joined the underground resistance movement and remained in Warsaw throughout the Nazi occupation. After the war, he became a cultural attaché at the Polish embassies in Paris and Washington. He defected in 1951 and lived for the next ten years in France.

In 1953, he published *The Captive Mind,* a shrewd and still unsurpassed analysis of the seductions of totalitarian rule for writers and intellectuals. This melancholy tale of how people of goodwill sold their souls made his name familiar to readers in the West. Milosz emigrated to the United States in 1961 and began teaching at the University of California at Berkeley. While his works were banned in Poland, he continued to write in Polish, refusing to shed one identity and language for another as many other exiles had done. In 1980 he won the Nobel Prize for literature.

If Milosz impresses us today as a man of uncommon clearheadedness in an age of Manichaean ideological passions, that's not how he was regarded fifty years ago by many of his Polish and Western literary contemporaries, who were either open or secret admirers of the Soviet Union and "people's democracies." What Milosz had to say about his experience of totalitarianism was of scant interest to them. "Nothing is more depressing," he wrote later, "than the sight of people who believe that they are following collective manias of their own free will."[1] These were the days when Sartre lauded civil liberties in Russia as incomparable and claimed that prison camps there, if they actually existed, were accidental, while they were an integral part of the capitalist system. Truth about Stalinism and the sufferings of people under Communism was not Sartre's great concern. Like many other writers and intellectuals, he wanted to be on the side of History, whose laws had suddenly become intelligible and could be manipulated to ensure a happy future.

"What is this monster, historical necessity, that paralyzed my contemporaries with fear?" Milosz asks in an autobiographical piece now collected in *To Begin Where I Am*. And his answer is Hegel's (and Marx's) Spirit of History. It is the same blind force that rules the cruel world of nature, in which everything that happens to us is predetermined. Our wishes count for nothing since its laws are beyond appeal. In short, individually we do not exist; only historical processes do. One cannot fight History, so one better shut up and submit to the inevitable.

Milosz did not. Only today can we fully appreciate how solitary and how heroic his resistance was. To steer one's way between the ideologies of the left and the right and keep one's integrity as much as one is able to was no small accomplishment in a century when so many others, who ought to have known better, behaved despicably. It was like "choosing between madness (a refusal to recognize necessity) and servility (an acknowledgment of our complete powerlessness)," he later wrote. Writing in *The Captive Mind* about the situation of the intellectual in Eastern Europe, he describes his own predicament and the reason for his exile as well:

> He has been deceived so often that he does not want cheap consolation which will eventually prove all the more depressing. The War left him suspicious and highly skilled in unmasking sham and pretense. He has rejected a great many books that he liked before the War, as well as a great many trends in painting or music, because they have not stood the test of experience. The work of human thought *should* withstand the test of brutal, naked reality. If it cannot, it is worthless. Probably only those things are worthwhile which can preserve their validity in the eyes of a man threatened with instant death.

After millions of deaths in that war, the reproach Milosz made to the arts was that they ignored or veiled the dark forces that were about to be unleashed. Even religion and philosophy were accomplices, pulling wool over our eyes to distract us from what was taking place. Milosz's chief complaint in the essay "Ruins and Poetry"—and it lies at the heart of all his literary work—is that much of literature in the West lacks a sense of hierarchy when appraising experience. It confuses what is important and what is trivial, making itself in the process frivolous and forgettable. All reality is hierarchical, he writes, because human needs and the dangers threatening people are arranged on a scale— say from a pinprick to mass murder. Whoever comes to realize the existence of that scale behaves differently from someone who has the luxury to disregard it. The poetic act, for Milosz, depends on the amount of historical reality in the poet's mind. One can claim, for instance, that a sonnet of Mallarmé's is a typical work of the nineteenth century, when civilization appeared to be something guaranteed. But how is one to write poems among the ruins and the stench of carnage of occupied Warsaw or any other city in the world yesterday or today?

You whom I could not save
Listen to me.
Try to understand this simple speech as I would be ashamed
    of another.
I swear, there is in me no wizardry of words.
I speak to you with silence like a cloud or a tree.
What strengthened me, for you was lethal.
You mixed up farewell to an epoch with the beginning of a
    new one,
Inspiration of hatred with lyrical beauty,
Blind force with accomplished shape.
Here is the valley of shallow Polish rivers. And an immense
    bridge
Going into white fog. Here is a broken city,
And the wind throws the screams of gulls on your grave
When I am talking with you.
What is poetry which does not save
Nations or people?
A connivance with official lies,
A song of drunkards whose throats will be cut in a moment,
Readings for sophomore girls.
That I wanted good poetry without knowing it,
That I discovered, late, its salutary aim,
In this and only this I find salvation.
They used to pour millet on graves or poppy seeds
To feed the dead who would come disguised as birds.
I put this book here for you, who once lived
So that you should visit us no more.

This poem comes from a sequence, "Voices of Poor People,"
published in the book *Rescue* in 1945. It already contains many
characteristics of Milosz's style. The language is plain and yet
supremely eloquent. He has no use for poetry that turns its back
on the public and seeks only aesthetic perfection. The Symbol-
ists' dream of distilling the language of the tribe into an elixir
of pure lyricism is for him at best a charming delusion. For
Milosz the high point in French poetry comes not with Mal-
larmé but with Apollinaire's "Zone" and Blaise Cendrars's
"Easter in New York," both published in 1913. He also approves
of Whitman, who influenced these two French poets and who

himself claimed that the great poets are known by the absence of tricks in their work. Milosz comments in a note to his long poem *A Treatise on Poetry* (1955–56):

> We sustain the existence of the realm of poetry only through daily effort. It is wrested from the world not by negating the things of the world, but by respecting them more than we respect aesthetic values. That is the condition for creating valid beauty. If it is obtained too easily, it evaporates.

In the century of diverse literary avant-garde movements and traditionalist backlashes, he was not afraid to promulgate what he calls "realistic poetics." For him, the mental act of securing a grasp on reality must precede the poetic act. "As I am, so I see," wrote Emerson. There's a hard, cold, sober side to Milosz's poetics that is almost classical. As far as he is concerned, the poet who refuses to face our tough and predatory reality is living in a fool's paradise. Seeing clearly is a moral issue for him. In his poem "Bobo's Metamorphosis" he praises a painter and disparages Zbigniew Herbert, his great Polish contemporary, who in a poem called "Study of the Object" says mischievously that the most beautiful object is the one that does not exist:

V

I liked him as he did not look for an ideal object.
When he heard: "Only the object which does not exist
Is perfect and pure," he blushed and turned away.
In every pocket he carried pencils, pads of paper
Together with crumbs of bread, the accidents of life.
Year after year he circled a thick tree
Shading his eyes with his hand and muttering in amazement.
How much he envied those who draw a tree with one line!
But metaphor seemed to him something indecent.
He would leave symbols to the proud busy with their cause.
By looking he wanted to draw the name from the very thing.
When he was old, he tugged at his tobacco-stained beard:
"I prefer to lose thus than to win as they do."
Like Peter Breughel the father he fell suddenly
While attempting to look back
between his spread-apart legs.

And still the tree stood there, unattainable.
Veritable, true to the very core.

Milosz is wary of the twentieth-century ethos that prescribes negation for poets. He objects to the numerous incarnations of Modernism, their linguistic experiments, their rebellion against the literature of the past, their loathing of both the middle class and the common people, and their conviction that our human life suffers from a fundamental lack of meaning. Mockery, sarcasm, and blasphemy are cheap when compared to the evil let loose in the world. The pressures of the times in which he has lived have made Milosz, he claims, write a different kind of poem, one that would leave a testimony of a radically different experience of what was until then known as reality. In his journals, he compliments American poets on their first-rate technique, but complains that they have nothing to write about in their tedious everydayness, free of historical upheavals. If there's no sense of history, he argues, there's no sense of the tragic, which is born of the experience of collective misery.

As much as I would like to agree with him about that, I cannot help recalling the many worthy exceptions. There's Whitman, for instance, who wrote magnificent poems about the Civil War, and then there's Emily Dickinson, a poet equally capable of a tragic view of life, who ignored that war entirely in her poems. Isn't poetry, as Milosz contends, also an exploration of our place in the cosmos? A number of American poets can certainly make a strong claim to have engaged in such exploration. It's a bad idea and a complete waste of time to prescribe what poets must or must not do because the best ones will always rebel and do the opposite.

"In spite of its great cruelties, I praised my time and I did not yearn for any other," Milosz writes in *To Begin Where I Am*. Anyone reading his *New and Collected Poems* expecting an unending landscape of ruins and sufferings is bound to be astonished by the delight he takes in nature. In his youth, he tells us, he safeguarded himself against grown-ups by his passion for his aquariums and his ornithological books. His early hero was the brave nineteenth-century naturalist, someone so ardent about collecting bugs that he completely forgets about his bride waiting at the altar while he climbs a tree in tails to catch a rare species of beetle with his top hat. Later in life, experience of the American countryside restored him, he tells us: "I plunged into books on American flora and fauna, made diplomatic contacts with porcupines and beavers."

In his poems and essays, however, Milosz also repeatedly proclaims his dislike of nature. He is astonished that its cruelties are usually regarded as "natural," as the wildlife programs on TV make evident with their images of mutual and indifferent devouring of various species. He is not insensitive, he assures us, to the beauty of mountains, forests, and oceans; nevertheless, nature, which is ever present in the imagination of American poets and often identified by them with reality, is nothing more for Milosz than a stockpile of clichés out of romantic pantheism. The wish to ascribe a benign will to the universe is an illusion. In one of his greatest poems, "To Robinson Jeffers," he addresses a poet who struggled with that question:

If you have not read the Slavic poets
so much the better. There's nothing there
for a Scotch-Irish wanderer to seek. They lived in a
    childhood
prolonged from age to age. For them, the sun
was a farmer's ruddy face, the moon peeped through a
    cloud
and the Milky Way gladdened them like a birch-lined road.
They longed for the Kingdom which is always near,
always right at hand. Then, under apple trees
angels in homespun linen will come parting the boughs
and at the white kolkhoz tablecloth
cordiality and affection will feast (falling to the ground at
    times).
And you are from surf-rattled skerries. From the heaths
where burying a warrior they broke his bones
so he could not haunt the living. From the sea night
which your forefathers pulled over themselves, without a
    word.
Above your head no face, neither the sun's nor the moon's,

only the throbbing of galaxies, the immutable
violence of new beginning, of new destruction.
All your life listening to the ocean. Black dinosaurs
wade where a purple zone of phosphorescent weeds
rises and falls on the waves as in a dream. And Agamemnon
sails the boiling deep to the steps of the palace
to have his blood gush onto marble. Till mankind passes
and the pure and stony earth is pounded by the ocean.
Thin-lipped, blue-eyed, without grace or hope,
before God the Terrible, body of the world.
Prayers are not heard. Basalt and granite.
Above them, a bird of prey. The only beauty.
What have I to do with you? From footpaths in the orchards,
from an untaught choir and shimmers of a monstrance,
from flower beds of rue, hills by the rivers, books
in which a zealous Lithuanian announced brotherhood, I
    come.
Oh, consolations of mortals, futile creeds.
And yet you did not know what I know. The earth teaches
more than does the nakedness of elements. No one with
    impunity
gives to himself the eyes of a god. So brave, in a void,
you offered sacrifices to demons: there were Wotan and
    Thor,
the screech of Erinyes in the air, the terror of dogs
when Hekate with her retinue of the dead draws near.
Better to carve suns and moons on the joints of crosses
as was done in my district. The birches and firs
give feminine names. To implore protection
against the mute and treacherous might
than to proclaim, as you did, an inhuman thing.

Milosz admires Jeffers's stubborn independence, his con-
tempt for the literary fashions of his day, and even his grumpi-
ness. He asks himself in an essay on the poet if he's like him,
and answers that he is not. He could not oppose, he says, the ter-
rifying beauty of nature to human chaos. Unmerciful necessity
is unacceptable to us. In the poem, he contrasts the simple peas-
ant culture of his homeland with Jeffers's blind cosmic force.
For him, as for Simone Weil, nature is neither good nor evil. We
crave to understand its purpose, and yet it eludes our interpre-

tations. We are torn between admiring some detail in it and wishing to make sense of the whole. In an essay on Lev Shestov, Milosz quotes with approval the Russian thinker's view that, since the Greeks, every philosophy has believed that only the universal is worthy of reflection. The contingent, the particular, and the momentary are the perennial spoilers of the vision of all-embracing Oneness—and that, come to think, is the reason for the age-old quarrel between poets and philosophers:

> The true enemy of man is generalization.
> The true enemy of man, so-called History,
> Attracts and terrifies with its plural number.
> Don't believe it.

中

Whoever wishes to know the kind of psychological and intellectual turmoil one goes through in difficult historical times will not find a more reliable or eloquent testimony than is to be found in Milosz's many books of poetry and prose, culminating in his ninetieth year with his selection of his finest essays, and with a book of almost 750 pages of new and collected poetry. It is hard to think of another poet in our day who could match the range and richness of his achievement. Milosz has a first-class mind and enormous erudition. He is the chronicler of the disenthrallment with the various "isms" that triumphed and then foundered in his and our lifetime:

> I think that I am here, on this earth,
> To present a report on it, but to whom I don't know.
> As if I were sent so that whatever takes place
> Has meaning because it changes into memory.

His work, with the exception of the few long poems, is extremely accessible, notwithstanding its often unfamiliar Polish and European setting. Poetry of ideas is frequently unbearable to read because the poet is not as smart as he thinks he is. Not Czeslaw Milosz. The brainier he gets, the more enjoyable he is to read. Among his many fine poems in that category I would single out *A Treatise on Poetry*, composed in 1955 and 1956. It's tightly written, witty, and simply dazzling. Many of his poems tend to hang together loosely, and that often turns out to be their strength. Donald Davie, in his book on the poet, makes an interesting observation about the insufficiency of the lyric to express our historical experience, registering as it does only the individual self.[2] A rich life, it turns out, can never be encompassed with a single point of view; for Milosz the quest for reality must include a mixture of styles, everything from didactic and narrative poems to a short lyric of just a dozen lines.

Milosz has been fortunate in his many excellent translators. This is true of both his prose and his poetry. Most of the poems in this book are the result of his collaboration with the fine American poet Robert Hass. I can't judge what they sound like in Polish, or what they lose in translation, but for the most part they read well in English, and in a number of instances they end up being magnificent American poems in their own right. Milosz has many styles, many voices. He describes himself as "a city of demons," and that must be the explanation for his large output. He says,

> The purpose of poetry is to remind us
> how difficult it is to remain just one person.

The effort of his best poems is not to arrive at a conception of reality, but to dramatize consciousness. His recurring theme is the endless quarrel the self has with itself and the world, its inability to resolve its contradictions while striving at the same time to arrive at some sort of affirming vision. Unfairly, I believe, he accuses Pasternak and others, like Beckett, of giving the impression that there is no alternative to helplessness. Even someone as unmodern as Frost is censured for his grim, hopeless vision of man's fate and for his skepticism and constant ambivalence. The imagination is a powerful antidote against anxiety, despair, the feeling of the absurd, and the other afflictions, Milosz has said, "whose true names are surely impiety and nihilism."[3] However, he is suspicious of imagination running wild. Poetry, as he conceives of it, stands against nihilism and is on the side of life. The moralist and the poet in him are often at odds. That poetry has little to do with morality, he finds deeply troublesome. In the very essence of poetry there is something indecent:

> a thing is brought forth which we didn't know we had in us,
> so we blink our eyes, as if a tiger had sprung out
> and stood in the light, lashing his tail.

That element of surprise is much more present in the poems of his old age. If I have a complaint about his earlier work, it is that he rarely lets his imagination take the poem to its own unpredictable end. The "blessed gift of spinning a tale out of a trifle" is how he describes that missing quality in a late poem. It cannot be done, alas, with the intellect. Milosz is one of the few poets who give the impression that they know what they will say before saying it in a poem, relying on his eloquence more than on the play of metaphors to make his meaning. Starting with the section of this book called "New Poems, 1985–1987," that is no longer the case. The poems are more and more the result of unexpected associations. He is still the poet of erudition and memory, surrounded by books of his favorite philosophers, theologians, and mystics, but now it is the small occasions in daily life that give rise to poems. Curiously, he ends by writing the kind of poem he once objected to in American poetry.

❧

How to tell *all* in the brief time one has? That is among the main worries of these later poems. They are often elegiac—as one would expect—and yet they are frequently cheerful. Lamenting and praising is what Milosz has always done. Yes, there is too much death in the world. Still, there's also the taste of strawberry jam, the dark sweetness of a woman's body, well-chilled vodka, herring in olive oil, bright-colored skirts in the wind, and paper boats no more durable than we are. "In advanced age, my health worsening," he begins a prose poem, "I woke up in the middle of the night, and experienced a feeling of happiness so intense and perfect that in all my life I had only felt its premonition." Even his most somber poems have a touch of that newfound happiness:

Abode

The grass between the tombs is intensely green.
From steep slopes a view onto the bay,
Onto islands and cities below. The sunset
Grows garish, slowly fades. At dusk
Light prancing creatures. A doe and a fawn
Are here, as every evening, to eat flowers
Which people brought for their beloved dead.

If you still don't believe that there's truth in poetry, go and read
Milosz, and you are very likely to change your mind.

NOTES

1. Czeslaw Milosz, *Beginning with My Street,* trans. Madeline G. Levine (New York: Farrar, Straus, and Giroux, 1991), p. 223.

2. Donald Davie, *Czeslaw Milosz and the Insufficiency of Lyric* (Memphis: University of Tennessee Press, 1986).

3. Quoted in Aleksandr Fiut, *The Eternal Moment: The Poetry of Czeslaw Milosz,* trans. Theodosia S. Robertson (Berkeley: University of California Press, 1990), p. 33.

The Mystery of Happiness

Of course, I never really believed it would happen. That I would grow old, I mean. I knew the unavoidable facts, saw the evidence all around me, but despite all that I went around as if it had nothing to do with me. (Frankly, even this year 2000 that is supposedly coming soon sounds fishy to me. I recommend a careful recount. Our world being the way it is, I bet somebody screwed up along the way.) Reality is very nice as an idea, but who wants to look at it in the face? In the course of my lifetime, I've watched a few people on their deathbeds, and they were not entirely convinced either. Secretly, we all hope that we are an exception to the rule. "You'll get caught," I remember long ago telling a couple of aspiring felons in my neighborhood who were planning to break into a garage that night and carry off tools and other equipment. How they laughed! How they pitied me! Their confidence was absolute; others may get nabbed, but not smart guys like us.

"You'll see when you grow up," someone is always advising us when we are young. In the days before cash machines were invented, when we went to our grandmothers for funds, we were obliged to sit and listen to their hard-earned wisdom. Everything was going to hell, the young people were getting more and more insolent every day, while in their youth sons still called their fathers "sir," and girls blushed at the mention of sex. I sat eagerly at the edge of my chair, nodding vigorously in approval, waiting for Grandma to click open the purse she was holding in her hands and count the small coins. I understood even then that censuring the new generation is one of the pleasures of old age. I didn't mind hearing for the hundredth time about all the disasters that befell members of our family who didn't listen to sensible advice like the kind I was getting, or about her various ailments requiring immediate medical attention and what the pea-brained doctor said on the phone when she finally got through to him . . . All that was fine and dandy, until that business about "seeing when I grew up" came around, and I stiffened, and couldn't wait to get the hell out of there. Poor grandma, what a pain in the neck she was. The sad truth is, she was right. With age, I do see things differently than I once did.

The reality of growing old didn't hit me until I was almost fifty. I woke up one morning a few days before my fiftieth birthday and suddenly grasped the enormity of it. A half a century is no joke. When I was already pulling our cat's tail, Hitler rode around in a car sightseeing in Paris. It wasn't the gray hairs on my head or the roll of fat around my middle that got to me, but the memories. I remember sitting in a first-grade classroom facing the pictures of Karl Marx, Stalin, and Marshal Tito hung high over the blackboard. My mother told me they were evil men, so I studied their faces carefully every day for little telltale signs. I remember the taste of American C-rations, long-forgotten brands of cigarettes, certain pop tunes and jazz standards when they were brand-new, and hundreds and hundreds of dead people no one probably thinks of anymore but me. So many faces returned that day, I was frightened. My head was a darkened theater where fleeting ghosts enacted brief scenes from their lives. The stage resembled an antique shop. How did I ever accumulate so much junk? I asked myself. It took me a while to get used to it—if one ever gets used to growing old.

In one of the last conversations I had with my father, he told me—or rather he told the hospital ceiling—that he had made one serious mistake in his life, one that he was truly sorry for. I perked up at once, expecting a Dostoyevskian confession, the story of some great wrong, a secret of a lifetime only to be revealed at death's door. In any event, he told me that he had made the error of following his doctor's advice when he was seventy. He had been counseled to stop eating sausages, salamis, bacon, tripe, suckling pigs, ham, headcheese, liver pâté, and other such necessities of life, and he had foolishly obeyed. For a couple of years he felt awful. How awful? I wanted to know. He was listless and mildly depressed, he replied. Then one day he came to his senses, started eating everything that was bad for him, and felt 200 percent better. He just regretted the years he wasted.

My father's dietary philosophy—which I mostly share—went this way: If it looks good on the plate and tastes good in your mouth, it must be healthy for you. The current view, of course, maintains the opposite: The more delicious it is, the sooner it'll kill you. Today in the United States the ideal is to lie in one's own coffin blooming with health. Still and all, I have to make a confession of my own. I can't eat as much as I used to. My old friends who remember my legendary appetite are crestfallen when they see how modestly I eat now. They recount to me the glories of my former gluttonies, and I listen to them with skepticism and mild disgust. It's true, I could eat a horse until recently and then ask if someone could please scramble a few eggs because I was dying of hunger. I still haven't learned true moderation, but in the meantime I'm getting picky. The older I get, the more fearful I am that the leaf of lettuce won't be crisp enough, the first sip of wine not quite what I hoped it would be. Can one generalize and say that one ends up by being the opposite of what one once was? In some instances, surely, but mostly not. For example, was there ever a case of a convinced pessimist becoming an optimist in his old age? Not unless he lost a few marbles along the way.

At the age of sixty-one, on certain days, I feel like a car with two hundred thousand miles on its speedometer. There's a knock in the engine, the radiator overheats, the body is rusty, the upholstery is ripped and stained, one windshield wiper doesn't work, the muffler is full of holes, and there's an oil leak. "Don't worry about it," my doc says. He insists I'm in fine shape despite high blood pressure, a touch of diabetes, and going deaf in one ear. He sounds to me more and more like a used-car salesman trying to unload a car that's been in a wreck, but what can I do? I listen to him like an easily fooled customer and speed away happy in a cloud of exhaust smoke, singing at the top of my lungs:

My momma told me
My poppa told me too
He said son
You are just living in a fool's paradise.

At three o'clock in the morning, after a night of tossing and turning, I'm not so cocky. I go squint at my unshaven face in the bathroom mirror and don't like what I see. Even Peter Lorre when he played the child murderer in that movie was more wholesome to behold.

Recently a reviewer squawked that my new book of poems is far too obsessed with death. He wondered why my books are getting gloomier and gloomier. The insinuation was, I ought to be more upbeat at my age, praising humanity and the eternal beauties of nature, dispensing serene wisdom as if I had a white beard, a white robe, and a cult following in California. Just you wait, snotnose, I said to myself, till you reach my age and start going to funerals once a month. What's there to be cheerful about? Every time you open the papers, the same murderous crooks are still in charge almost everywhere, the massacre of the innocent is still in full swing, while the primary intellectual effort of our literati is to conceal the fact that we haven't had a new idea in more than fifty years. Nobody tells you that stuff when you're young, and even if they bother to, it's in one ear and out the other.

Experience of a lifetime—let's not kid ourselves—is basically worthless. No one else is particularly interested in it, and why should they be? Since solitude is our true destiny, the only use we can make of our accumulated knowledge is to torment ourselves with it. Yes, after a certain age, it's always three o'clock in the morning. Sooner or later, everyone ends up having his or her own personal Grand Inquisitor. (Incidentally, black is no longer the required attire.) Tonight mine wears a pink bikini, dark shades, and is painting her nails red as she sits with legs crossed surrounded by various diabolic implements of torture. She may look like Lolita, but her questions are downright mean.

"To what do you attribute how your life has turned out? Certain historical events? The first poem you ever read? The ladies?"

"I've been racking my brains for years."

"And what about God?"

"I say, thank God there is no God to see me like this!"

"What about the devil?"

"I watched him give a press conference on TV yesterday."

"You are not making any sense, wise guy. How can you believe in Satan and not in Almighty God, and plus have the nerve to go around crossing yourself every chance you get?"

"I don't give a damn for your theological consistency. I'm just giving you my best hunch. Besides, I have too much on my mind. I have more worries than President Clinton does, and we know how much trouble he has had. You don't see me going around grinning at everything and everyone with my piling debts, my worries about children in faraway cities, worries about my poems being drivel, worries about drinking too much, worries about some cat taking its sweet time to return home at night, worries about going gaga, forgetting one day soon even my own name, shuffling around hunchbacked and toothless with pee-stains on my underwear. It's not just a few metaphysical problems I have to solve every night; I also need to figure out how to pay for the new roof on my house."

Once she stops pestering me, I steal a peek at the clock. Holy smoke, it's already quarter to five. They say time goes faster after you pass sixty. I believe it. Where are the indolent summers of youth when I moped from morning till night unable to think of anything interesting to do? I recollect pacing around my room in Oak Park, Illinois, repeating with greater and greater conviction, "Life is boring." In those days, the clock barely budged, the minute hand took long naps before it deigned to stir again— just to spite me! You fool, I'm thinking today, that was pure bliss. The mystery of happiness was in the clock. Time graciously stopped for you; eternity like a new lover threw open a door to a room you never suspected was there, a room leading to other rooms, airy and full of lazy, golden sunlight. You fiddled and diddled on the threshold and—horror of horrors—breathed a sigh of relief when the door shut in your face and the hand of the clock moved on.

The Romance of Sausages

Even their names are poetry to me: chorizo, merguez, rosette, boudin noir, kielbasa, luganega, cotechino, zampone, chipolata, linguica, weisswurst—to name just a few. Whose mouth has not watered in a well-stocked butcher shop or fancy food market at the sight of many varieties of sausages, fresh and smoked, stuffed with pork, beef, lamb, liver, veal, venison, poultry, and seasoned with herbs, garlic, pepper, and spices too numerous to count? Until about ten years ago, there was a small store specializing in regional French sausages on Rue Delambre in Montparnasse, that famous little street where at one time Isadora Duncan lived, Man Ray had his first studio, and Hemingway met Scott Fitzgerald in a bar called Dingo's. Each time I entered that shop, I experienced a surge of emotions as if I were about to lose control of myself and make a scene. I'd point to one kind of sausage, change my mind and point to another, then ask for them both. After they were already expertly wrapped and I was on my way out, I often rushed back and bought a couple more varieties. My visits were a year apart, but the owners remembered me well and approached me each time with a smile of recognition and a touch of apprehension.

"They are bad for you," some of my friends warn me when I confess to them my sin, as if all that stands between eternal life and me is one nicely grilled, richly seasoned andouillette. Sad to say, there are people who regard lovers of sausages as living in a kind of nutritional Dark Ages, ignorant of cholesterol counts and caloric intake. For them all those Italians, Greeks, Hungarians, North Africans, Chinese, Germans, and Portuguese frying, grilling, boiling, and poaching happily are living terribly mis-

From *The Poetry of Sausages*, in *Food and Wine,* June 2000.

guided lives. They have the highest esteem for native cuisines, but sausages are where they draw the line. Don't you know the disgusting things they put in them? they say to me incredulously after I appear unconvinced. Of course, I know. Some of the oldest and wisest cultures on earth eat them, is my defense. In France there's even an organization called the A.A.A.A.A.—the Amicable Association of Appreciators of Authentic Pork Tripe Sausages. A group of upright citizens, I imagine, who regard the sausage "made with pig's intestines filled with strips of choice innards mixed with pork fat and seasonings " to be the one and only ideal. In Finland, there is a similar society, whose members meet once a week to conduct what they call "sausage tests" while sitting naked in a sauna.

A sausage served in a restaurant of distinction can be an unforgettable occasion. An impeccably attired and dignified waiter has just uncovered a plate on which lies a lone wild-boar sausage next to a sprig of parsley. It is a joy to behold, and the first nibble doesn't disappoint, and yet, something is not quite right. A sausage feels more at home at a carnival or in a steamy kitchen. Sausages are sociable. A hot Tunisian lamb sausage will get along just fine with a potato from Idaho. A good-looking chicken leg, tentacles of a squid, and green peas from the garden are equally swell company. Portuguese, who love to combine odd ingredients in their cuisine, make a stew of pork, linguica, and little-neck clams. Sausages are the true multiculturalists. A large, mixed, and rowdy company makes eating them even more memorable.

My old buddy Bob Williams, in Hayward, California, used to make Italian sausage and peppers to perfection. He'd invite five or six people, give us a few bottles of good Zinfandel and even better Chianti, and take his time with the food. Finally he'd pour some olive oil in a frying pan in the kitchen just so our noses would know something was happening. Then, in due time, the onions would go in so the excitement could really begin. Before putting in the sausages, he'd bring them out to us so we could feast our eyes on them and grow hungry in anticipation. Supposedly, a Neapolitan guy in Oakland who didn't speak a word of English made them from an old family recipe. I never believed this story entirely, but such stories seem to be obligatory among cooks who serve sausages. There's always some ethnic in a small grocery store or a luncheonette in some outlying suburb or inner ghetto who sells the best sausage you ever tasted.

Indeed, by now Bob's sausages are beginning to send tantalizing smells our way, and everyone is rushing to pull up a chair to the table. Even a couple of elegant women who by their appearance eat nothing but baby vegetables are fighting for the bread in an unseemly hurry. Bob is carrying in a basket of freshly picked hot peppers from the garden for us to munch on, so that we can grow red in the face, gasp with astonishment at the wallop they pack, and gulp wine like water while listening to the sausages make their cheerful music on the stove. Since this is a confession, let me admit it: Italian sausages can be a big disappointment. They tend to be overdone, the peppers burnt, the onions likewise. It's all about timing, faultless timing. The accumulated experience of the cook in an inspired moment creates a small masterpiece in a frying pan impossible to repeat exactly.

In a country where almost everyone is continuously on a diet, the sight of so many sausages arriving on the table is always a shock. Despite his cherubic appearance and his broad smile, Bob makes me think of the devil in some medieval miniature dangling a tempting morsel before a saint kneeling in prayer. "Oh, how wonderful, but not for me! " a few of the company protest, quickly following that solemn announcement with, "Well, perhaps, maybe, just a tiny, little taste," as they reach with their forks. No one is waiting to be served. There's not enough bread, and the sausages are vanishing before our eyes as if they are part of a magic act. A bit of grease has fallen on a pale yellow silk blouse, but its owner doesn't care. She's laughing with her mouth full. A sudden, horrible realization is on everyone's mind: *I love sausages. I'll kill for another sausage.* "Keep them coming," we are shouting to Bob, who is back in the kitchen, and he's more than happy to oblige.

Poetry: The Art of Memory

It all depends on how one looks at it. It's either a blessing or a curse to be a poet in the Holy Land, a place with so much history, so much myth and religion. As far as Yehuda Amichai was concerned, it was like being ground between two grindstones, or like living next door to God. Every time he opened his eyes, the biblical past was there. Where once miracles were performed and prophets fell down struck by some vision, there were now traffic jams and crowded beaches. Tradition for an American poet is something one seeks in the library. For Amichai in Jerusalem, it came with his cup of morning coffee and the first look out of the window.

"Lovely is the world rising early to evil, " he writes in an early poem, because there's that too. The endless cycle of wars, massacres of the innocent, and the inevitable despair that comes with it. What is amazing about Amichai is how levelheaded he stayed to the very end, balancing his philosophical gloom against a lust for life. Was there a greater love poet in the last century? I can't think of one. "A psalmist," Anthony Hecht called him. Even when he played the role of an amused observer of human folly, he praised left and right. His visions of happiness have a modest, human scale. White shirts and undershirts on the laundry line mean for now there is peace and quiet here.

Even when he was a young poet, he wrote about death. First-generation Israeli, born in Germany in 1924, immigrated in 1936, there was something unsettled in him, as if his parents' migration had not yet quieted in him. His subject was always himself, poetry as an ongoing journal of one's reaction to the

From *Tin House* 2, no. 3 (2000).

world. Memory and forgetting were his constant preoccupation. Everything came down to that. The miracle that someone remembers, the unthinkable horror that we all forget. Amichai was a wise man who wanted to remind us of our hearts. The clarity of his poems is a testimony to his humility before the immense task. He wrote lyric poems because there are moments in every life that must not be lost. Who will remember the rememberers? he asked. We, who read and love his poems, will.

Evil: Menus and Recipes

Oh those awful Serbs! Until recently no one cared or knew much about them in the West, and now almost everyone has an opinion about them, and it's most likely to be unfavorable. Karadzic and Mladic—icons of inhumanity—are taken as the embodiments of the soul of their people. Even before the wars in the former Yugoslavia started, American newspapers were offering analysis of the Serbs. A *New York Times* editorial on April 4, 1989, for instance, described Yugoslavia's Roman Catholic republics as "the country's most advanced and politically enlightened regions," now undeservedly threatened with "bullying" by a block of Orthodox Christian republics. It was an open-and-shut case: a struggle between industrious Roman Catholic Slavs, whose culture and traditions are a part of the civilized Europe, and the Byzantine East, where laziness and violence are the rule. Later on, during the war in Bosnia, it was the Bosnian Muslims who were praised for their affinity with the West and for being unlike Muslims elsewhere.

Before long Western newspapers and Balkan nationalists were using much the same language. On all sides, the enticement of making indiscriminate generalizations about ethnic groups proved to be irresistible. With complete assurance, editorials, columns, and op-ed pages purported to locate characteristics that have supposedly been present for centuries in these little-known Balkan peoples. For many Western commentators, talking about the Serbs was a way of defining their own cultural superiority. Without any serious knowledge of the area and its history, they offered crude morality plays for their readers' edification, conveniently overlooking the possibility that their own

From the *London Review of Books* 19, July 31, 1997.

diatribes resembled the nationalist rhetoric they so deplored. Most absurd of all was the idea that there were two kinds of nationalism: the "postmodern nationalism" of Slovens and Croats, tolerant, democratic, and nonaggressive; and the Serbian variety, which is intrinsically expansionist, authoritarian, and violent. To anybody able to read the nationalist press in Serbia and Croatia this is laughable. The best proof of the fact that the Serbs and Croats are one and the same people is the almost identical idiocies their super-patriots spew out every day.

Once it was clear that the West agreed with the local nationalists that the peoples of the former Yugoslavia had nothing in common, it followed that the breakup of the country was something to be encouraged. The inconvenient fact that the Serbs were the largest ethnic group, and the only one with significant numbers scattered throughout the other republics, was never seriously addressed. Instead, they were dismissed as the jailers of Yugoslavia, the perennial troublemakers, the sort of people who couldn't be reasoned with, who didn't understand anything more subtle than the carrot and the stick.

Even the new Croatian constitution—as Tim Judah points out in *The Serbs,* his fine book on the history, myth, and destruction of Yugoslavia—which demoted six hundred thousand of Croatia's Serbs to minority status by making the new country the "national state of the Croatian people," was not sufficiently alarming as to postpone its recognition. The journalists cheering the separatist republics said repeatedly that the Serbs' fears were wildly exaggerated, as if they themselves would take in stride the news that they were no longer American citizens, but were from now on members of an Irish, Hebrew, Chinese, or other minority in an Anglo-Saxon–only state. If the Serbs had complaints, it was said, they should have worked within the system. Even when thousands were fired from their jobs merely for being Serbs, and the streets and schools named after the heroes of the antifascist resistance were renamed after the fascist responsible for the mass killings of Serbs in World War II, they were supposed to hold their breath and wait for Susan Sontag or Bernard Henri Levy to take up their cause.

It is important to understand that even if Mahatma Gandhi had been the president of Serbia there would still have been a

Serbian problem to solve. Yugoslavia made sense for the simple reason that neither Christ nor Allah would be able to draw just borders between most of its peoples. Once the country was officially abolished by the international community, the position of the Serbs, and of all those who regarded themselves as Yugoslavs, became impossible. One day they were free to drive to Italy with their families; the next, their documents were worthless and they no longer knew of what country they were citizens.

Tim Judah's book *The Serbs* is the first detailed and reliable guide to these complicated questions, alert to the pressures of Balkan history and completely impartial: nationalists on all sides will loath it. The first part is devoted to a summary of Serbian history since the Middle Ages, and the remaining two-thirds to recent events. In Judah's summary, Serbian history is an unhappy tale of wars, massacres, occupations, and migrations. Ethnic cleansing, according to Judah, was what every side did in the region over the centuries, so what they set out to achieve this time around was not an aberration but part of a long local tradition. I'm not so sure. Nationalists turn to history in search of a license to kill, and even academics are inclined to attribute large-scale evil to ethnic and cultural causes. The implicit premise here is that you and I have a hidden bond with those who murder in our name. A far more plausible explanation is that the tragedy in Yugoslavia was caused by men who were the product of fifty years of Communism rather than of any native tradition.

At the point of the breakup of Yugoslavia, the Serbs faced three options, all equally unworkable: (1) a rump Yugoslavia without Slovenia, reconstituted as a loose confederation of democratic republics, which, given the Communists turned nationalists in power everywhere, including Serbia, was not about to happen; (2) a Yugoslavia broken up into five or six independent states, which would mean leaving a large number of Serbs in Croatia and Bosnia and Herzegovina reduced to minority status; (3) all Serbs in one large, new state—which would in turn make everybody else a minority. If there had been no bad blood, perhaps a solution could have been found. But given the massacres in World War II, it was impossible not be concerned about the future. "Every village in Croatia and Bosnia," Judah writes, "was now beginning to remember what the neighbors had done fifty years before. If they were not actually plotting revenge, they began to prepare, as best as they could, against the possibility that their neighbors might be doing so." Like many others, I kept hoping that mutual self-interest would prevail, forgetting that this wasn't a situation in which anything so rational could be expected. "We don't wish to live with them anymore. We have to separate once and for all," one read and heard people saying in Serbia, but nobody I heard or read gave any clue as to how this could be achieved fairly and peacefully—and, of course, it never could have been. It was no more sensible than the old idea that Alabama and Mississippi could be turned over to African Americans. Would New York City cab drivers and doctors jump at the opportunity to live in a ghetto among their own people? The nationalist program was as stupid as that.

In this supremely difficult moment, the Serbian people made a catastrophic mistake. They allowed a cynical opportunist, the corrupt Communist Party, and the powerful secret police to take charge of their national interests. The rise of nationalism and the dismemberment of Yugoslavia postponed an assessment and the full understanding of the totalitarian establishment. Serbian society did not have a reprieve to formulate what it means to be a free citizen and not a subject. Communism had made ethics a forbidden subject, and so did the nationalists. The consequences of a near-total destruction of civic values were never acknowledged. Overnight, the same mafia that had deprived the people of their freedom for fifty years changed tack and began to promise them the restoration of their dignity, and their rights, and the people bought it. Most Serbs bridle when they hear this. As Judah points out, "Not only were people disoriented but, brought up with an heroic image of themselves as the people who had opposed fascism unlike the Croats, they simply refused to believe the most appalling camp stories." They still imagine that the dreadful bias against them in the Western media somehow cancels their own responsibility for what happened in the war. They point to the shamefully under-reported atrocities committed by Croats and Muslims, as if these excused their own murders. They hate to be told that their rulers do not have their best interests at heart, preferring to lay the blame on a global conspiracy or the duplicities of the New World Order.

Judah's book makes plain the convergence of competing ambitions, the monstrous alliance of incompetents, opportunists, and criminals bent on enriching themselves while supposedly defending the holy cause of the Serbian people. "It was not just expelled Muslims and Croats who were robbed," he writes. "Local industrial and agricultural assets that would have helped sustain Serb-held areas both during and after the war were simply stripped and sold off." As long as there were fortunes to be made, no one in charge was in a rush to stop the carnage. One of the drawbacks for those who preach democracy in the Balkans is that democracy is not as profitable as nationalism.

Despite his own evidence to the contrary, Judah nevertheless accepts the claim that there was also an attempt to realize the centuries-old dream of a Greater Serbia. I don't believe this for a moment. Serbs have never had a clear-cut national program. I'm fifty-nine years old and have had innumerable political discussions with Serbs of every description, but the subject of Greater Serbia has never come up. We are more likely to make fun of our national pretensions. My fondest memories of my grandfather are of him inventing funny and bawdy versions of medieval heroic ballads. Scarce as they sometimes appear to be, there *are* Serbs who understand that they are a small people living unenviably at the crossroads of three religions and several contending empires. The opposition daily and weekly papers have published hundreds of pieces in recent years pointing out that the idea of "Greater Serbia" was nothing but a half-baked scam, a "plan B" set out after Milosevic's other schemes to extend his power over the rest of Yugoslavia had collapsed.

The question that remains is how something so mad and self-defeating as ethnic cleansing, destruction of cities and villages, and massacres could have occurred. How, to echo Judah, could Serbian history be so misused? As with most such outrages, there's no single explanation. It started with the state-controlled media in all the former republics. Give some ideologue a monopoly on the means to fan hatred between ethnic groups in the U.S.A., and don't be surprised when neighbors begin killing neighbors and justifying their actions with tales of ancient victimhood. In Yugoslavia the old Communist propaganda machine was already in place, expert at manufacturing internal and external enemies and uncovering hundreds of conspiracies. All that was necessary was a change of vocabulary. It didn't take much to convert class warfare into ethnic hatred and have the intellectuals start making excuses for a new round of crimes. The truths, half-truths, and plenty of lies—who could sort them out? Pretty soon even sensible people could not tell them apart.

And where was the democratic opposition all this time? The problem, as has often been the case with the Serbs, was that they were suicidally divided. During World War II, they were more or less evenly split between royalists and Communists. At the same time as they were being slaughtered by the hundreds of thousands in Croatia, they were engaged in killing each other in a civil war. These animosities have not died out. The coalition of opposition parties, which functioned so well last winter when the demonstrations were taking place, has now practically fallen apart. One side, still hoping to bring the monarchy back, accuses the other of being crypto-Communists. And if that were not enough, the Serbs are also split regionally: the different histories and cultures of Serbia-proper, Montenegro, Vojvodina, Bosnia, and Herzegovina sometimes make it seem that contemporary Serbs live simultaneously in different centuries. Given the complexity of the situation and the lack of unity, Milosevic had a pretty free hand. He made secret agreements. The first one was with the Slovenian president to let Slovenia leave the union. In 1991, while the war in Croatia was still in progress, he made the all-important deal with Tudjman to split Bosnia and Herzegovina between them. In order to implement that plan, Milosevic continued to arm the Serbian population in Bosnia and Herzegovina, as he had previously armed the Serbs in Croatia, and instructed his secret police to organize "patriotic" paramilitary groups to go into Bosnia and do whatever they could to encourage the Muslims to flee. "Milosevic organized everything," says Vojislav Seselj, the leader of the Serbian Radical Party:

We gathered the volunteers and he gave us special bar-
racks . . . all our uniforms, arms, military technology and
buses. All our units were always under the command of the
Krajina or (Bosnian Serb) Republika Srpska Army or the JNA.
Of course I don't believe he signed anything, these were ver-
bal orders. None of our talks was taped and I never took paper
and pencil when I talked with him. His key people were the
commanders. Nothing could happen on the Serbian side
without Milosevic's order or his knowledge.

The Serbian paramilitary had plenty of company. This is how
Judah describes the scene in Bosanski Brod in the days before
the war started in Sarajevo:

Gunmen and militias from a multitude of groups prowled
around town. A number of Muslims from Serbia's Sandzak re-
gion had "Allah is Great" stitched to their arm flashes. They
said they were in training for the struggle that they intended
to take to Serbia itself. Croats from the Croatian Army were
also in town, some sporting the "U" symbol of the old Ustasha
state.

The strangest aspect of the whole story is that the massive ex-
changes of population received tacit support from abroad. In
the West, enthusiasts of the breakup had their own ideas about
drawing new borders. Yugoslavia was to be abolished and di-
vided between spheres of influence, except for Bosnia which
was to become a kind of theme park where all religions and eth-
nic groups would live happily ever after. In the last months of
the war, the ethnic cleansing in Krajina, Srebrnica, and Western
Bosnia took place with a nod from Washington and the go-
ahead of the local leaders, as no one any longer doubts.
    Clearly, to be an individual in the former Yugoslavia, some-
one who minds his or her own business, who has no intention
of harming anybody, has become an extremely precarious busi-
ness. The nationalist euphoria did not include everyone. Thou-
sands of Serbs deserted in the war, and even more left the coun-
try. Muslims had even less choice. They ran for their lives. My
parents, like so many others, went through something very like
this more than fifty years ago. To their absolute astonishment,

they found themselves on the other side of the globe through no fault of their own. I figured this wouldn't happen again in my lifetime. I never expected to see my childhood replayed on CNN. It is the predicament of the innocents on all sides that makes the story of Yugoslavia so awful. If you forget them, you end up exonerating Milosevic, Tudjman, and Izetbegovic. The West, by dealing only with the nationalist leaders, has effectively made travel arrangements for anyone who holds different views.

This may be perfectly obvious, but long experience has taught me that not all innocents have the same status. In 1948 my mother, brother, and I were deported from Austria by a pro-Tito English colonel who lectured us that we had no right to leave a country run by workers. In the present war, Croatia cleansed its territory of most of its Serbian population with only a few mild rebukes from the West. Being accepted as an innocent victim has always required that one be a member of a fashionable victim group.

There was nothing inevitable about the tragedy in Yugoslavia. Religion, cultural determinism, national traits are just pretexts. The nationalists everywhere are forever trying to embroil the rest of us in their genocidal projects by raking over the coals of history. They reject the possibility of any kind of choice, believing instead in the iron law that says we must either kill or be killed.

Morality Made Easy

> Begun in folly, continued in crime, and ended in misery.
>
> —Erasmus

It's hard to find anything good to say about Serbs these days. Even when fourteen farmers are massacred gathering the harvest in their fields on what was surely a beautiful, warm summer night, the kind of night when one forgets about war, we say to ourselves, after taking in the full horror of it, what did you expect? No one ever should die like that. Burning villages, killing women and children, and chasing hundreds of thousands of blameless folk out of their homes has lethal consequences. To set neighbor against neighbor is not only evil; it's like cutting off one's own nose to spite one's face. Poor Serbs—their leader is a Jim Jones and they the members of a religious cult preparing themselves for mass suicide for the last ten years. The poison they've been sipping is a foul-smelling brew of bluster and self-pity. *We defended Notre Dame and the honor of Viennese ladies against Asiatic hordes, and now all you Europeans have turned against us.* Like any such spectacle of self-delusion, this is painful to watch. So many perfectly normal and good people held hostage by these crazies on all sides. How did they ever get into this mess?

Predicting Milosevic's actions has always been child's play. One merely had to stop and consider what would be of benefit to Serbian people and then imagine its opposite. "Is he going to do something really vile to the Albanians?" I wondered with a couple of Serbian friends as the NATO bombs were starting to fall. We were speechless at the prospect, the horror awaiting the innocent, and the shame we felt as Serbs. "Of course, he's going to

From "Who Cares?" in the *New York Review of Books,* October 21, 1999.

do it," we agreed after a moment's reflection. When it comes to Slobo, prophets of doom are right every time.

There are Serbs who still see no connection between the actions of their president and their national calamity. Unfortunately, Serbia is a country where too many people have closed their eyes to nine years of hideous carnage and destruction wrought in their name, a place where the truism that you reap what you sow has become incomprehensible. The Serbs are never wrong because there's always someone else to blame. In a state where a large special police force modeled after Tonton Macoute and a ruling elite have been practicing mass murder and plunder for years, academicians, intellectuals, and political analysts continue to bewitch themselves with Machiavellian intricacies of the thousand-year-old conspiracy against the Serbs who, if truth were only known, have never made a single child cry anywhere. In essence, they are arguing that the world's objection to Srebrenica is philosophical, that the accusation of genocide is just another instance of the bias against Eastern Christianity. It's no wonder Serbs are held in such contempt.

Milosevic's dream has come true. Serbia is now a nation of ten million war criminals. Yes, Serbs are stupid scum, he must think. Even abroad they have said that. He only has to read the Western press to have his corroboration. Haven't a few of their finest intellectuals, historians, and political analysts said that there's no such thing as an innocent Serb? That's what he himself always believed about Albanians and Bosnians. His disagreement with the rest of the world, it turns out, is a mere quibble about the correct name of the ethnic group. The doctrine that underlies his policies in Bosnia and Kosovo and the one that makes all Serbs culpable are identical.

Collective guilt and collective punishment were evoked repeatedly during the bombing of Serbia in the media to justify the death of civilians and the destruction of the economic infrastructure, even in towns and cities held by the opponents of the dictator. The 600,000 Serbian refugees from Croatia and Bosnia and some 179,000 from Kosovo who are now in Serbia and Montenegro are similarly regarded without pity. The figure for Serbian war deaths in the last ten years is unknown. According to the *Washington Post* it is over 150,000 just in Bosnia.

There's little interest in how these people perished, as if their deaths were perfectly excusable and forgettable. The view that blameless people everywhere deserve compassion is clearly a belief only a simpleton or a poet could hold. Our moralists are choosy. Not every ethnic cleansing deserves that name. These epicures of human suffering know how to best choose and savor the deserving mother and child among the masses of the unhappy. They are lucky not to be able to read Milosevic's press. The same selective morality is on the menu there.

This similarity of outlooks drives anti-Milosevic Serbs to despair. To realize that Western figures you once idealized hold thinly disguised totalitarian views while supposedly raging against fascism is pretty shocking. Being intellectually independent in Serbia has always been difficult. *If you don't love the smell of our collective shit, you're not one of us,* is the nationalists' message. They regard people of integrity as paid traitors, and a day doesn't go by without some politician or general threatening prison or worse. Milosevic is routinely compared to Hitler in the West, and yet his opponents, who have been enduring all sorts of risks and have stood up against naked force and evil, are not revered as heroes but painted with the same brush. Daniel Jonah Goldhagen's book *Hitler's Willing Executioners: Ordinary Germans and the Holocaust* was repeatedly evoked in the United States to hint that Serbs may be another "genocidal people." Anyone in the media who could bring in another example of the bottomless depravity of the Serbian national character was cheered on. Every lunatic nationalist figure in their history with a racist agenda, no matter how marginal, was exhibited as being representative of the entire people. The massacres of the Serbs were always unproven, their expulsions always voluntary, their national interests nonexistent, their nationalism uniformly virulent and dishonorable, their history a pack of lies, their Ottoman occupiers broad-minded multiculturalists and themselves victims of centuries of Serbian ingratitude.

And how did the new Balkan experts come to these far-reaching conclusions? Did they spend long hours in the library researching the subject? Of course not. There's a quicker and far more impartial way to do these things. Here's a tip: if you want to get the straight goods about anyone, just go ask their neighbors.

These assertions went unchallenged, so as not to upset the often eminent author who without knowing a word of the language pretended to have an uncanny ability to tell what other dark secrets lurked in the soul of every one of these willing executioners of Milosevic. The Serbs in the opposition who could have answered these charges with authority and credibility were not welcome, since in addition to correcting the many factual errors and preposterous claims of the self-appointed expert, they would inevitably have reminded the author of his or her nation's ample history of slaughter and hatred. We in the United States, for instance, easily forget that we are also nationalists who grow indignant when the seamy side of our "Manifest Destiny" is mentioned. Despite all that, this truncated view of the Serbs and their past will remain in circulation for a long time, if not forever.

In the meantime, the Albanians are back in their burnt homes in Kosovo returning the favor by burning Serbian and Gypsy homes, looting, kidnapping, and doing plenty of bloodletting of their own. It turns out that they, too, believe in collective guilt and punishment. As William Pfaff explains in the *Herald Tribune*, "As Bismarck observed, nations are created in blood and iron. Such is the case of Kosovo." In other words, don't lose sleep over it, folks, if the Albanians practice a little fascism of their own.

The Serbian refugees camp by the side of the road or in abandoned buildings in Serbian border towns and wait for a handout. The Yugoslav government allocates one deutschemark per day to those expelled from Croatia and Bosnia, so there's not much they can expect. If they travel to Belgrade to plead their case, the cops beat them, since Milosevic doesn't want a public reminder of his disastrous policy. If they seek medical help or attempt to enroll their children in local schools, they are turned back by the authorities, since, of course, they do not exist. On a rare occasion, a foreign journalist stops to interview them and finds them living without hope in appalling conditions. To his or her astonishment and great annoyance, he or she also discovers that they don't feel any collective guilt for the crimes committed in Kosovo. What's worse, they still dislike the Albanians and the United States, so forget about feeling sorry for them, even though half are children under sixteen years of age. As the Chinese proverb says, "The weak are always without honor." Everyone always expects the poor and homeless to have higher standards of behavior than we ourselves have. The presumption in many of these articles is that the journalist comes from a community where blind prejudice and intolerance are completely unknown. What starts as an attempt to describe some unfortunate family's plight ends up being a heartfelt testimony to the peerless virtue of the reporter.

Let's not kid ourselves: parading one's superiority is what truly matters. The notion that ethical decisions are difficult, full of ambiguities and contradictions, is just too much of a hassle. It makes one stay up nights. Even then, the decision reached leaves one unsatisfied in the morning and worried that some wrong has been overlooked somewhere. Morality made easy, on the other hand, is like a diet book claiming that one can eat all one wants and still lose a whole lot of weight. In other words, lessons in virtue for everyone else and no painful scrutiny of one's own conscience is the ideal. And don't forget, the farther away the injustice, the louder your voice must be.

"Blessed are those who got nothing, because they ain't gonna get nothing," I heard a radio preacher say once. We can be pretty sure that total misery awaits these Serbian refugees now that we are patting ourselves on the back for winning this war. If they are nearly invisible now, they are bound to become even more so in the months to come. United Nation relief agencies and the Red Cross do what they can, but the chances of Christiane Amanpour or Elie Wiesel dropping by for a visit, or the international community providing major aid, are slim. Even the bombs that fell on the refugees and killed more than a few did not upset anyone very much. Now even their fellow Serbs are trying to ignore them in a country where the economy is destroyed, unemployment is at 50 percent, the land and water are polluted by the toxic fumes of bombed chemical plants, and the food is unsafe to eat. I cannot imagine a more awful predicament, but then I remember the Kurds, the Palestinians, and so many others in Africa who are also in very bad shape. What makes the plight of these Serbs different, perhaps, is that their displacement occurred at a time when everyone talks about human rights. The wars against Milosevic were ethical and humanitarian campaigns intended to rescue the innocent. How is it then that these thousands of refugees are not an issue for the high-minded among us who pretend to be the moral conscience of our time?

Metaphysician of the Little Box

It may turn out that the most interesting literature in this century did not come from the various movements under the broad label of Modernism and the great literary centers, but was the work of outsiders and mavericks starting with Kafka, who created something really without a precedent out of a mix of native and foreign traditions. The poetry of Vasko Popa, who died in 1991, is of that eccentric company. He was the most translated and the best-known Yugoslav poet in the twentieth century. As far back as 1969, Penguin first published his *Selected Poems,* with an introduction by Ted Hughes, in its series on modern European poets. Popa was then usually grouped with Zbignew Herbert and Miroslav Holub, two other astonishingly original East European poets. Their work was plainly unlike anything being written in England and the United States at that time. In Popa the reader encounters an exotic blend of avant-garde poetry and popular folklore, thinking this is what the poets from that part of the world are like. Actually, no Serbian poet sounds like Popa. He was both the product of his time and place and the inventor of his own. This, as we'll see, is one of the many paradoxes about him.

Popa was born in 1922 in an area north of Belgrade called Banat whose population was a mixture of Serbs, Germans, Slovaks, Hungarians, and Rumanians. His father was a record clerk in the village and afterward a bank employee, and his mother was a housewife. He attended elementary and high school in the town of Vrsac, where he graduated in 1940 and where as a teenager he started writing. In the last year of school

Review of *Collected Poems of Vasko Popa,* trans. Anne Pennington, rev. Francis Jones. From the *London Review of Books* 21, no. 6 (March 18, 1999).

he discovered Marxism and continued to think of himself as a Marxist for the rest of his life. The war began for Yugoslavia on April 6, 1941, when the country was attacked simultaneously by German, Italian, Bulgarian, and Hungarian armies and quickly occupied. Nevertheless, in the fall of that year, Popa, following his parents' wishes, went to Bucharest to study medicine. He left after one year to go to Vienna and read philosophy. On a visit home in May of 1943, he was arrested and interred in a concentration camp in a nearby Zrenjanin, where he remained till September. How his release was arranged, I've no idea, but he did return to Vienna where he now enrolled in classes on French and German literature and also worked as a streetcar conductor. He did not return to Vrsac again till just after the liberation. There he promptly joined the Communist Party and shortly afterward moved to Belgrade to become a student of French language and literature at the university. This was a most unusual travel itinerary for wartime years, as even his party dossier at the time suspiciously pointed out. In Belgrade, Popa began his literary career editing and writing for a weekly literary paper and eventually became an editor at the prestigious publishing house where he would remain till close to the end of his life.

The appearance of his first book of poems, *Bark*, in 1953 created an uproar even before its publication. Critics and poets of the dominant socialist-realist persuasion, who had already seen the poems in the literary journals, attacked Popa. One typically demanded, "How is it possible that such texts can be written by a young writer and published by a renowned literary magazine?"—implying, of course, that there was nothing Communist about the poems. The age demanded paeans to the struggle of the working classes and got avant-garde poetry instead. Others griped about Popa's hermeticism. For instance, even the title of the book is ambiguous. In Serbian "bark" can mean both the bark of a tree and bread crust. Nonetheless, a few critics and writers supported Popa, writing polemical pieces explaining the poetry and in the process undermining the aesthetic principles of their opponents. Popa was the luckiest of young poets: from the day he started publishing, no one ever remained indifferent to his poetry.

The poems in *Bark* were written between 1943 and 1953 and were continuously revised up till the 1969 reissue. The first edition had a number of prose poems that were in time discarded. What remains today are four cycles of poems. They serve as a kind of preamble to Popa's corpus. Many of the peculiarities of his poetry were already present. The poems are short, but arranged in sequences, giving the individual cycles a quasi-narrative quality. On one hand, as even his early critics saw, the poems have a conciseness and formal rigor that are almost classical, and on the other hand, one finds in them a wildness of metaphor that equals anything the Romantics and the Surrealists ever dreamed up. Except for this first book and his last one, Popa is usually absent from his poems. Here, however, the inner torments of a young man in love are an issue. One of the cycles, "Far within Us," is a sequence of erotic poems in the tradition of Breton and Éluard.

The subject of another cycle, "Besieged Serenity," is the existentialist drama of one man's confrontation with the absurd. Camus's Sisyphus, with his "universe henceforth without master," is a dead ringer for the hero of these poems. The breach between the self and the world is the issue. "How to live without being torn between these infinities? " Popa writes in one of the few short notes he left on poetry. What interests him is the dignity and the heroic forbearance of the everyman-Sisyphus pushing his rock, or—as Saul Steinberg wittily has it in a old cartoon—pushing a huge, boulder-like question mark, up a hill.

The poems that elicited the most controversy when the book came out were in the cycles "Landscapes" and "List." Here's one of them:

On the Table

The tablecloth stretches
Into infinity

The ghostly
Shadow of a toothpick follows
The bloody trail of the glasses

The sun clothes the bones
In new golden flesh

Freckled
Satiety scales
The breakneck crumbs

Buds of drowsiness
Have burst through the white bark

Surrealist nonsense, the reviewers said. There were poems about a plate, a chair, a potato, an ashtray, a hatstand, and other such unpoetic things. The critics were right in blaming the French. It was the Surrealists who discovered the inanimate object charged with mystery in the midst of our commonplace reality. However, where Breton, Éluard, and Peret sought to create in the reader a state of heightened lyricism with a bombardment of unrelated and outrageous images, Popa, despite his flights of fancy, remained focused on the object. The riddle-like poems in his "List" are basically descriptions. He is the most intellectual, the most self-conscious of poets. It's the phenomenology of the imagination as it engages the world that he is primarily interested in.

I suppose there are three types of poets: those who write without thinking, those who think while writing, and those who have figured out everything before they sit down to write. The first group is the largest and the last the smallest. As a young poet, when I met Popa in 1970, poetry for me was still pretty much a spontaneous venting of some inner turmoil. Poetry is a visionary activity, my Romantic and Symbolist masters assured me. In a moment of inspiration, one somehow stumbled upon extraordinary images and metaphors—and that was that. These notions of mine both amused and annoyed Popa. He did not believe in chance. He compared the poet to a miner, a pearl hunter, a lighthouse keeper, or someone assembling a watch. For him the poem was an act of supreme critical intelligence. There were strict rules as to what was permitted and what was not. The poet labored within the confines of the long tradition of poetry and within the idiosyncrasies of the language in which he or she wrote. The poet was both fettered and free. Good poetry was made not by teenagers in love, but by sly old tricksters. Popa himself had already thought out everything that he was going to write for the rest of his life. Late one night, after much wine, he described to me in ample detail his future poems. I assumed that this was just wine talking, but not so. In the coming years, I'd see his poems come into print, and they were pretty much as he had described them that night.

His second book of poems, *Unrest Field,* which came out in 1956, again had four cycles of poems. This time, however, the poems were unmistakably original They were fun to read despite the fact that their meaning was not always easily dislodged. Wallace Stevens's observation that we often admire something long before we understand it pertains here. The cycle called "Games" is the most famous among them. Some of the games Popa played are familiar, and some are his own invention: the Nail, the Seducer, the Wedding, the Rose-Thieves, the Seed, Leapfrog, the Hunter, Ashes.

The one called Hide-and-Seek goes this way:

> Someone hides from someone
> Hides under his tongue
> He looks for him under the earth
>
> He hides in his forehead
> He looks for him in the sky
>
> He hides in his forgetting
> He looks for him in the grass
>
> Looks for him looks
> Where he doesn't look for him
> And looking for him loses himself

We associate games with childhood and innocence, but that's not how it goes here. Popa's players are types; their roles are fixed. The games they play are intense and all-consuming, but their aim is obscure. In these grim nursery rhymes, pain and suffering are real. The creator of the games, the one who first made us play, is absent. These are the circular games of hell played with broken toys, as Ivan Lalic said. They are obviously emblematic of our lives. We go on playing them in the hope that they make sense despite our suspicions to the contrary. For Popa, the biggest joke of all is that there is no joker in the pack.

The cycle "Give Me Back My Rags" personifies that unknown

jokester and attempts to exorcise its power. The anonymous speaker of the poem rebels and refuses to play the game:

> Damn your root and blood and crown
> And everything in life
>
> The thirsty pictures in your brain
> The fire-eyes on your fingertips
> And every every step
>
> The three cauldrons of cross-grained water
> Three furnaces of symbol fire
> Three nameless milkless pits
>
> Damn your cold breath down your gullet
> To the stone under your left breast
> To the cut-throat bird in that stone
>
> To the crow of crows the nest of emptiness
> The hungry shears of beginning and beginning
> To heaven's womb don't I know it
>
> Damn your seed and sap and shine
> And dark and stop at the end of my life
> And everything in the world

Here the translation does not do justice to the spirit of the original, and how could it? The phrase "give me back my rags" comes out of poor children's games and has numerous connotations. Girls play with scraps of old material, swapping them and reimagining them into clothes for their dolls, until they quarrel with each other and want them all back. The entire cycle is that kind of pretend-game, built out of idioms and the submerged and multiple meanings that lie lurking in them.

Every one of Popa's cycles is a self-contained universe, in which the end is also a beginning. The model is the cyclical, sacred calendar of myth. The idea is to spin the wheel of metaphors and images until sparks of associations begin to fly for the reader. Poetry conceived that way is a kind of alchemy since its object is to transmute matter into spirit.

"Writing is primarily an experience of language," Robert Creeley said of himself, and this is equally true of Popa. He reaches back to the folk tradition of riddles, charms, proverbs, nursery rhymes, and exorcisms for clues as to how to make poems. What Popa is after are the eyes and ears of the anonymous folk poet who could hear flowers growing, the hen lay its eggs, the stars multiply, the earth and the sun speak with a human voice. "Father's scythe lies across mother's Sunday skirt" is how a Serbian riddle describes the crescent moon. "What runs but never walks" is a river. "If not for the wind, spider webs would cover the sky" is another saying.

"A metaphor is a memory of the Golden Age when all was everything," Andre Sinyavski says somewhere in his journals. Popa sought the origins of myths in certain colloquial turns of phrase, and he looked for them in oral literature. Writing about an early twentieth-century poet, Momcilo Nastasijevic, who was his biggest influence and someone with similar ideas about the uses of native tradition, he praises the poems by saying that each one is a "verbal icon of our immaculate mother tongue." Poetry's task is to remember the archetypes, recover the symbols, discover the laws of their transformation, not by studying mythology or dictionaries of symbols, but by hearing, as if for the first time, the language that comes out of our mouths:

> You speak to the wall. You speak into the dark. You speak into the fire. You speak to the monsters in your dreams. You speak to your own death. You speak to her death, speak to death. You speak to water. Speak to nothingness, speak into nothing.

In this short note on poetry, Popa asks about authentic language. The pressing question is what words one would trust today. What words did our ancestors use? There are key words, he believes, words that open worlds, words that are already a poem. How does one find these words? His answer is that "you go to meet the words bringing your gifts—your attentiveness and your silence." This would be just abstruse, pseudo-mystical twaddle if the poems did not make it happen. "Plato located the soul of man in his head; Christ located it in the heart," St. Jerome said, and Popa found it in the very language we speak.

What his translators are compelled to do accordingly ends up being a kind of magic operation. One plucks English idioms out of a hat, as it were, and keeps the ones that hint at the lushness of the original. As a translator of Popa myself, I can vouch that this is a very tricky business. Anne Pennington wisely observes: "English literary usage is too far removed from our folk tradition to mingle with it happily; literary Serbo-Croat was found as recently as the early nineteenth century and was firmly based on the spoken language and popular culture." Unfortunately, in the case of "Give Me Back My Rags," what is also missing from her translation is the teasing tone of the original and the cumulative effect of that voice.

There's another important ingredient of Popa's poetics, and that is the comic. It fully comes to the fore in his third book, *Secondary Heaven* (1968). Writing about humor in the introduction of an anthology of Serbian poetic humor, which he compiled, he speaks of it as the supreme transgressor, the prankster who mixes the sacred and the profane and makes heaven and earth change places. Such humor allows us to see how everything would look if it were different while at the very same time it does not permit us to rest there. In other words, this humor is as unruly as poetry and as dangerous as truth.

Here, for instance, is Popa's comic version of how the world began from the cycle "Yawn of Yawns" in that volume:

A Forgetful Number

Once upon a time there was a number
Pure and round like the sun
But alone very much alone

It began to reckon with itself

It divided multiplied itself
It subtracted added itself
And remained always alone

It stopped reckoning with itself
And shut itself up in its round
And sunny purity

Outside were left the fiery
Traces of its reckoning

They began to chase each other through the dark
To divide when they should have added themselves
To subtract when they should have added themselves

That's what happens in the dark

And there was no one to ask it
To stop the traces
And to rub them out

In another poem in the same cycle, "A Conceited Mistake," he imagines the creation of the world as an accident: a small, silly error that invented space and time because it could not bear to remain alone with itself. *Secondary Heaven* is a book of many such speculations. The poems read like creation myths of some lost tribe. The entire book is made up of playful conjectures on the various ways cosmologies are invented and mirror our human foibles. As above, so below, is the axiom. Our intelligence and our foolishness are mutually dependent.

His next two volumes of poems are very differently conceived. The poems in *Earth Erect* (1972) address specific events, historical monuments, and heroes and symbols of the Serbian tradition. There are cycles about St. Sava, the national patron saint, and pilgrimages to various monasteries; the battle of Kosovo is there too, and so is the first uprising against the Turks. Since Popa believed that a poet's imagination is intricately tied to the language and place he came from, this was not an unexpected development. He may be charged with being a cultural nationalist, but certainly not a political one. There's nothing fanatical or exclusionary about his view of Serbian history and culture.

Wolf Salt, published in 1975, is made up of seven cycles on the lame wolf, the old pre-Christian Serbian tribal god whose memory continues to live on in stories, cults, legends, and rituals. The poems pay homage to this ambivalent figure of good and evil, life and death, extinction and survival, the ancestral spirit of his people. Ted Hughes, in his introduction to the *Collected Poems,* compares them to psalms. That is true. The poems celebrate the figure of the lame wolf, but also pray to it to reveal the secret of changing a stone into a cloud, the cloud into a deer with gold antlers, the deer into a white basil flower, and so on forever. Above all, these are psalms to poetic metamorphosis.

After its appearance, some read *Wolf Salt* as a nationalist work. Popa was praised in Serbia and rebuked elsewhere in Yugoslavia.

This is unfair. No nationalist in Serbia has ever mentioned these poems, as far as I know. Popa was too subtle a thinker to be accused of jingoism. The last time I saw him, in 1989 in New York, he was extremely worried about what the nationalist crazies and opportunists were cooking up. "There'll be bloodshed soon," he told me with complete confidence. With his Rumanian background, he could see clearly that he was already a suspect in the eyes of super-patriots. That's how vile and stupid these people are. No poet ever had such a profound and keen involvement with the Serbian tradition.

Raw Flesh (1975) and *Cut* (1981), his last two published books of poems, are more personal. The first-person pronoun returns. These are autobiographical and occasional poems of great directness and charm. They sound like short magic-realist anecdotes, something one would find in Marquez's *One Hundred Years of Solitude:*

The Lost Red Boot

My great-grandmother Sultana Urosevic
Used to sail the sky in a wooden trough
And catch rain-bearing clouds

With wolf-balms and others
She did many more
Great and small miracles

After her death
She went on meddling
With the business of the living

They dug her up
To teach her how to behave
And to bury her better

She lay there rosy-cheeked
In her oaken coffin

On one foot she was wearing
A little red boot
With splashes of fresh mud

To the end of my life I'll search
For that other boot she lost

As a translator of this poem and many others in the book, I naturally have many reservations about individual word choices and admiration for others. Popa employs a more motley diction than Pennington offers. She is far more formal and unvaried than Popa, who is capable of verbal dazzle that makes him sound at times like Paul Muldoon. Francis Jones, who expanded and revised the *Collected Poems,* is aware of the problem. He says: "His words and images are multilayered, combining concrete representations with idiomatic, proverbial and atavistic meanings to form complex, archetypal signs, which interpret more levels of existence than what is merely tangible in this or another universe." Popa, who knew Paul Celan and admired his difficult poetry, often came pretty close himself to being untranslatable. Despite these quibbles of mine, what the late Anne Pennington and Francis R. Jones have accomplished here is a true achievement and deserves our gratitude.

Popa died without completing another one of his long-term projects, a book that was to be called *Iron Garden.* Only one cycle, "The Little Box," was finished and published in his lifetime, while parts of four others and a few isolated poems were included in a posthumous volume. The workings of his magical box resemble the workings of the imagination, that mother of all mythologies. In Popa's metaphysics, reality was not invented by the imagination; its meanings were. When we give the box a shake, religions and philosophies, with their assorted gods and devils, pop up. Imagination is a mixed blessing. It works both for us and against us. We cannot resist its temptations, and yet its activity has a way of undermining everything we know. Hasn't this been what poetry has always secretly been up to?

Last News of the Little Box

The little box with the whole world inside
Fell in love with herself
And conceived inside herself
Another little box

The little box's little box
Fell in love with herself too
And conceived inside herself
Another little box

And so on ad infinitum

The little box's whole world
Should be somewhere
Inside the little box's last box

None of the little boxes
In the little box in love with herself
Is the last one

Try finding the world now

When I once mentioned to Popa that none of his views struck me as being Marxist, he just gave me an exasperated look, as if there was no way for me to understand—and I did not press him. If anybody ever managed to reconcile revolutionary and religious temptations in our time, he certainly did. He was the kind of poet he was because of the many contradictions in his life. Poetry with its own many delicious paradoxes came to the rescue.

Self-Portrait with a Bowl of Spaghetti

I don't require a hypnotist to recover the memory of the first bowl of spaghetti I ever ate in my life. I came to Italian food late. My grandmother and mother made noodles and macaronis, but nothing else that could remotely be described as Italian. In my mother's family, garlic and olive oil, two of life's peerless delights, were regarded with horror, as something people of suspect ethnicity and class coated their food with. It was on a pizza pie that garlic in obscene quantities first entered our home. As for spaghetti, it may have been served in a bowl, but it came out of a can bought at the supermarket. True, my father would once in a while bring home a bottle of Chianti, some Genoa salami, and provolone cheese, but these he mostly consumed alone with his own thoughts since my brother and I were hesitant to share in this ritual of his which my mother openly disapproved of. With my parents' marriage collapsing, I did not realize when I moved away from home at the age of eighteen that I was eventually going to find a surrogate home in Italian restaurants.

In August 1956, I found a job at the *Chicago Sun-Times* and a small apartment near Lincoln Park. I had a high-school diploma, but no money to go to college except at night. I ate mostly in greasy spoons until a fellow I worked with took me to a Chinese restaurant and eventually to an Italian one. Before I go any further, let me point out the obvious. Waiters and waitresses make all the difference in Italian restaurants. They are curious. Who's this kid eating with such a huge appetite and always leaving a good tip? They banter with you and comment on the dishes you order. In time they become your professors in what is going to be a lifelong study. Since I was only in kindergarten, I learned about

From *Self-Portrait with Spaghetti*, in *Food and Wine*, October 2000.

such basics as garlic bread, green and black olives, anchovies, minestrone, lasagna, veal parmesan, sausage and peppers. I was a teacher's pet, you may say, willing to try anything and liking everything I tasted. If I was flush, I would order a second plate of spaghetti with meatballs, to the delight of the waiter and the owner. In those days, gluttony was still regarded as a proof of robust health. The basic philosophy was, the more you ate, the happier you were. I didn't need convincing. I went back to my Italians every chance I got.

After I moved to New York in 1958, I lived in seedy hotels and furnished rooms in the Village and worked at various odd jobs, everything from being a bookkeeper to selling shirts in a department store. At first, since I was short of funds, I passed my lonely evenings roaming the streets and reading the menus of Italian restaurants in the area. Most of them served the usual fare, but there were one or two places with tantalizing, unfamiliar dishes—fried artichokes, linguine alla vongole, sautéed calf's liver—I was going to try as soon as I had money. I have a distinct memory of being asked by a courtly, elderly waiter if I wanted my spaghetti "al dente" and thinking he was suggesting a sauce named after the great Tuscan poet of heaven and hell. The waiter, Guido, who became another mentor, was wary of my enthusiasm, until my ardent desire to be initiated into the mysteries of capers, funghi porcini, tripes, squid, and the glories of Barbaresco and Barolo wines could not be doubted anymore. It took me years to reach the high-school level in Italian gastronomy and begin to dream of university. As I ate my way into higher wisdom, I also learned about the culture that came with the food. "Italian restaurant" is really a misnomer, since Italy is a land of many distinct regional cuisines. That knowledge came to me piecemeal. Bolito misto, for instance, that delicious dish of boiled beef, veal, sausage, and potatoes which I ate in a place on Thompson Street, came from northern Italy, and spaghetti carbonara from Rome. Then there was the music. One heard operatic arias and popular songs if there was a radio, a jukebox, or a portable record player behind the bar. As often happens in Italy, one says to oneself happily in such moments that this is how life ought to be.

I made most of these discoveries alone. The hard-drinking crowd of painters and poets I hung out with at the Cedar Bar, the White Horse, and the San Remo had little interest in fine cooking. With me, the more I drank, the hungrier I became. Also, I preferred wine to whiskey and gin. In those days hardly anyone else did. I remember badgering people, even offering to pay so we could go out and eat. Women were more impressed if you took them to a French restaurant uptown. Nevertheless, we were all likely to end up in my favorite Italian place, where I would tell them the story of how Marcel Duchamp, in his early, impoverished years in New York, would eat for lunch every day a bowl of plain spaghetti with butter and cheese accompanied by a glass of red wine. Perfect, I thought.

Italian restaurants produce not only epicures but also aspiring cooks. I bought cold cuts, cheeses, and olives for years in Italian groceries on Bleecker Street until one day I started cooking pasta, grilling sausages, and inviting friends over to my place on East Thirteenth Street. In the 1950s and 1960s almost no one in literary circles knew how to cook, so these modest efforts of mine received extravagant praise. From then on, each time I tasted something in a restaurant, I'd wonder how it was made, what spices were used, and recollect other occasions when the same dish had come out differently. Living in a small village in New Hampshire as I do now and cooking Italian is a way of carrying on that comparative study. This may be a tautology, but a meal that does not cause an outpouring of memories is not a memorable meal. I don't know how other poets imagine their muses, but my muse is an Italian cook. Give me a bowl of spaghetti, and I'll write you a poem.

The closest I can get to authentic Italian food now is a place in Portsmouth called Anthony Alberto's, where I can have a fine meal and be inspired. I've had many happy moments in my life eating or thinking about what I was going to eat. Going to a restaurant is always an adventure. An unforeseen, mouthwatering *something* may lie in store. Reading the menu at Alberto's one night, it struck me that it sounded like a passionate, lascivious declaration of love. I went home and wrote a poem—or more accurately, I shut my eyes and imagined a menu:

My chicken soup thickened with pounded young almonds.
My blend of winter greens.
Dearest tagliatelle with mushrooms, fennel, anchovies,
Tomatoes and vermouth sauce.
Beloved monkfish braised with onions, capers
And green olives.
Give me your tongue tasting of white beans and garlic,
Sexy little assorment of formaggi and frutta!
I want to drown with you in red wine like a pear,
Then sleep in a macédoine of wild berries with cream.

It is their unhurried air that makes most Italian restaurants congenial to everything from flirting to a rambling philosophical discussion. You linger over a glass of red wine and a plate of cheese at the meal's end, alone or in the company of friends, while the place empties. Outside, there may be the lights of Manhattan or the tugboats in Portsmouth harbor. The waiter or the owner may bring a grappa eventually to remind you of the lateness of the hour, but they do not rush you. Hell! You may as well have another round, this time insisting that they join you, and of course, they are most likely to agree.

Poets Wary of Poetry:
Billy Collins and James Tate

1

I remember overhearing a conversation at the conclusion of a poetry reading many years ago. Two very funny poets had read that night, Russell Edson and Bill Knott, who were in top form and had the audience laughing. "Weren't they just great?" a woman said on the way out, and her companion agreed, "Yes, they were." Then, he paused for a moment and added, "Of course, you know, that was not really poetry." It shocked me to hear him say that. He meant, I suppose, that poetry is serious and what these fellows had just given us was an evening of light entertainment. Probably, if he had been pressed to explain himself further, he would have argued that solemnity is the indication of weighty subject matter, while comedy at best is a pleasant diversion with no edifying lesson to teach. Of course, he is not alone in feeling that way. Let the poet mention the eternal beauties of nature, and most readers are under the impression that something sublime is being said. Let him mention a hot dog on a bun, and everybody knows instantly that this man will never be Dante.

Anyone who thinks he knows what poetry is and takes the trouble to read widely in books and anthologies of the last forty years is bound to be infuriated. What one finds in them are poems based on such clashing ideas of poetry that if one were asked to point to a typical American poem of the period, one

---

From "I Know Where I'm Going," in the *New York Review of Books*, February 28, 2002.

would have a hell of a time deciding what that is. There was a time in the 1950s and 1960s when the various poetic movements had labels and clearly defined positions to set them apart. There were the so-called Confessional poets, the Beats, the New York poets, the Deep Image poets, and the Black Mountain poets. With their clannish loyalties, they resembled Mafia families, only they fought their wars in literary magazines rather than in the streets. There were a few independent poets who kept their own counsel, but most of the poetry being written at the time could be characterized as belonging to one of these groups. Such fierce commitments to a single aesthetic program weakened in the 1970s. Poets started to shop around. Mixing poetic styles as if they were ethnic cuisines is the rule today.

Readers and critics of poetry tend to have far less wide-ranging taste than poets do. They have their own notion of what is "poetic" and what is not. The possibility, which contemporary American poetry amply demonstrates, that one can write good poems from radically different premises strikes them as nonsense. They believe in the eternal recurrence of the one true tradition throughout the ages to which all great poets pay homage. They may be right about that in some general way, except that's not how it works in practice. The whole idea of the "poetic" is far more a historical variable than a definable and timeless property. Poets themselves are certainly of two minds about that. There are those who seek to give authority to their work by deliberately acknowledging an aspect of that tradition, and there are those who yearn to slip out of its clutches entirely. The problem with any tradition is that it is also a storehouse of dead metaphors and clichés. As the late poet William Matthews observed some years ago, most of the poems one reads in literary magazines can be reduced to the following:

1. I went into the woods today and it made me feel, you know, sort of religious.
2. We're not getting any younger.
3. It sure is cold and lonely (a) without you, honey, or (b) with you, honey.

4. Sadness seems but the other side of the coin of happiness, and vice versa, and in any case the coin is soon spent and on we know not what.

Paradoxically, what has given American poetry its originality is this very suspicion of the "poetic," combined with an extraordinary belief in poetry's visionary powers. For both Billy Collins and James Tate, two poets only superficially alike, a poem presents an opportunity to get away from poetry. Never seen before, never heard before is what they hope for. They trust their comic sense to defend them against hackneyed rhetoric. As far as they are concerned, it is better to be accused of playing the fool than to be caught setting up the props and wearing the old costumes of some literary fashion.

2

Billy Collins, who was appointed poet laureate of the United States in June 2001, is an amazingly successful poet who did not publish his first book until he was past forty and whose book sales for a number of years now have quietly surpassed those of any other living or dead poet in this country. That a serious poet is widely read is a wonder to both his publishers and the press, who tend to write about him with the incredulity that would greet the discovery that Elvis Presley composed symphonies and string quartets in secret.

Collins is fun to read, and modern poetry on the whole, despite much evidence to the contrary, is supposed to be incomprehensible. Nor does he shy away from imagination and stick to some version of plodding realism. He has absorbed all the Modernist techniques and uses them well. In fact, what surprised me reading his selected poems, and what I had not noticed reading his individual collections over the years, is how self-consciously literary he is. Was it Novalis who said there is something astonishing in finding oneself writing a poem? That appears to be Collins's predicament too. Here, for example, is how some of his poems start:

A sentence starts out like a lone traveler
                                ("Winter Syntax")

Even if it keeps you up all night,
wash down the walls and scrub the floor
of your study before composing a syllable
                                ("Advice to Writers")

The column of your book titles,
always introducing your latest one,
looms over me like Roman
architecture
                                ("The Rival Poet")

I ask them to take a poem
and hold it up to the light
like a color slide
                                ("Introduction to Poetry")

There are other poems in the selected poems that deal with
poetry: "Lines Composed Over Three Thousand Miles from
Tintern Abbey," "American Sonnet," "Taking Off Emily Dickin-
son's Clothes," "Splitting Wood," which takes after Frost, and
one called "Monday Morning" that echoes Stevens's "Sunday
Morning"—and that's not all of them. Collins is like a jazz mu-
sician quoting snatches of other tunes in his solo. He is telling
the reader, I'm hip and you are hip. I will demystify poetry for
you by letting you in on a secret. Even poets think poetry can be
pretty silly at times. As Marianne Moore said, "Reading it, how-
ever, with a perfect contempt for it, one / discovers in / it after
all, a place for the genuine." Collins, who has a well-stocked lit-
erary mind and is not ashamed to show that he does, nonethe-
less shares her suspicion.

&

In the course of writing many poems, every poet ends up by con-
structing an identity which we as readers, gullible as we are, take
to be his or her real self. We hate to think that all that supposed
honesty might be a pose, a literary confidence trick to make one
sound believable. In his recent and very funny *Paris Review* in-

terview on the art of poetry, Collins says: "I try to start the poem conversationally. Poems, for me, begin as a social engagement. I want to establish a kind of sociability or even hospitality at the beginning of a poem. The title and the first few lines are a kind of welcome mat where I am inviting the reader inside." Collins comes across in his poems as a slightly eccentric but friendly neighbor, a professor with a nice wife in some affluent suburb or small town, who walks his dog and does the usual errands and chores associated with that kind of life. He likes jazz, good food, a good story, and is doubtless someone you would love to spend an evening with. Probably one of the reasons for the success of his books is that he gives the impression to his readers of being like them. If they were ever to write poems, they think, this is how they themselves would write them.

Consolation

How agreeable it is not to be touring Italy this summer,
wandering her cities and ascending her torrid hill towns.
How much better to cruise these local, familiar streets,
fully grasping the meaning of every road sign and billboard
and all the sudden hand gestures of my compatriots.

There are no abbeys here, no crumbling frescoes or famous
domes and there is no need to memorize a succession
of kings or tour the dripping corners of a dungeon.
No need to stand around a sarcophagus, see Napoleon's
little bed on Elba, or view the bones of a saint under glass.

How much better to command the simple precinct of home
than be dwarfed by pillar, arch, and basilica.
Why hide my head in phrase books and wrinkled maps?
Why feed scenery into a hungry, one-eyed camera
eager to eat the world one monument at a time?

Instead of slouching in a café ignorant of the word for ice,
I will head down to the coffee shop and the waitress
known as Dot. I will slide into the flow of the morning
paper, all language barriers down,
rivers of idiom running freely, eggs over easy on the way.

And after breakfast, I will not have to find someone
willing to photograph me with my arm around the owner.

I will not puzzle over the bill or record in a journal
what I had to eat and how the sun came in the window.
It is enough to climb back into the car

as if it were the great car of English itself
and sounding my loud vernacular horn, speed off
down a road that will never lead to Rome, not even Bologna.

"Consolation" is a tongue-in-cheek poem in praise of the
virtues of staying home. From the details provided, it is clear
that the narrator has been to Europe. Being a tourist doesn't re-
ally sound like such a horrible ordeal, but since he can't go
there this summer, he may as well make the best of staying
home. Here at least, he reminds himself, one can eavesdrop on
people and relish the local idiom. The point made is not new.
Frost, Stevens, W. C. Williams, all argued along these lines for
their refusal to become expatriates in the 1920s. If that red
wheelbarrow glazed with rainwater beside the white chickens is
not as interesting as a street scene in Paris, then there is no
hope for American poetry.

&

"I want to start in a very familiar place and end up in a strange
place," Collins says in that same *Paris Review* interview. My
complaint is that he doesn't do this often enough in his selected
poems. Despite all the funny and clever turns along the way, too
many poems have predictable conclusions. One drawback of
satire is that it has an agenda. It knows where it is going. Collins
is so much in control that by the end of a poem I'm left with the
feeling that I've been told everything that there is to know. Such
clarity in a poet is admirable, but as Collins himself realizes,
there has to be a countercurrent, a touch of ambiguity and un-
certainty, as it were. Not the kind that leads nowhere and makes
the reader give up on the poem in no time, but the kind that
draws us back into it. What one needs is some unexpected
image or twist in the point of view that makes us realize that
there's more here than meets the eye. When that occurs, as in
the following poem, when he seems to be surprising himself as
much as he is surprising us, Collins is by any measure a very fine
poet:

Afternoon with Irish Cows

There were a few dozen who occupied the field
across the road from where we lived,
stepping all day from tuft to tuft,
their big heads down in the soft grass,
though I would sometimes pass a window
and look out to see the field suddenly empty
as if they had taken wing, flown off to another country.

Then later, I would open the blue front door,
and again the field would be full of their munching,
or they would be lying down
on the black-and-white maps of their sides,
facing in all directions, waiting for rain.
How mysterious, how patient and dumbfounded
they appeared in the long quiet of the afternoons.

But every once in a while, one of them
would let out a sound so phenomenal
that I would put down the paper
or the knife I was cutting an apple with
and walk across the road to the stone wall
to see which one of them was being torched
or pierced through the side with a long spear.

Yes, it sounded like pain until I could see
the noisy one, anchored there on all fours,
her neck outstretched, her bellowing head
laboring upward as she gave voice
to the rising, full-bodied cry
that began in the darkness of her belly
and echoed up through her bowed ribs into her
gaping mouth.

Then I knew that she was only announcing
the large, unadulterated cowness of herself,
pouring out the ancient apologia of her kind
to all the green fields and the gray clouds,
to the limestone hills and the inlet of the blue bay,
while she regarded my head and shoulders
above the wall with one wild, shocking eye.

As selected poems go, *Sailing Alone around the Room* is not a big book. The poems date back only to 1988. Accordingly, Collins's range is not great. One cannot really speak of his early and his late work. He has the same anxieties about poetry and his readers early on as he does in some of the final poems in the book. Just as that becomes a little annoying, he will turn around and write some exquisite lines and then an entire poem. "The Brooklyn Museum of Art," "The Dead," "The History Teacher," "Nostalgia," "Sunday Morning with the Sensational Nightingales," "The Blues," and "Serenade" are first-rate. It's difficult not to be charmed by Collins, and that in itself is a remarkable literary accomplishment.

3

James Tate, who was born in 1943 in Kansas City, Missouri, has been a very prolific poet. I count thirteen major collections and two books of prose since his first volume, *The Lost Pilot* (1967), won the Yale Series of Younger Poets Award. This doesn't include dozens of small-press books that he brought out in the late 1960s and 1970s, all wildly experimental. He has received just about every prize that we give our poets, everything from the National Book Award to the Pulitzer Prize for his *Selected Poems* (1992), and deservedly so. And yet, despite his many honors and a large following, there has been very little critical writing on his work. This comes as a surprise since there are full-length studies written on much younger and less substantial poets. Tate has made himself difficult to classify by writing many different types of poems, from straightforward lyrics in fairly plain style to poems so thick with images and metaphors that they are nearly unparaphrasable. The way the critics usually cope with him is to call him a Surrealist or a Dadaist and leave it at that. Unquestionably, like many other poets of his generation, Tate read the French and Latin American Surrealists and under their influence filled his poems with poetic images that seem to defy all laws of literature and common sense. Nevertheless, his taste for the absurd and the comic is purely American. If Tate is a Surrealist, he belongs to that native strain to which Mark Twain, Buster Keaton, and W. C. Fields also belong.

The comic sense and poetic imagination have much in common. They depend on juxtaposition of unlikely elements, the joining of two distant realities whose resemblance has not been grasped till that very moment. In Tate's poems nothing is stable. The sudden eruption of metaphor is the only reality, and that reality keeps changing. The poet is at the mercy of his imagination. He is a comic anti-hero seeking shelter in a house of cards his metaphors built. He knows his predicament is absurd; he also knows it's exhilarating. That devil-may-care quality is already present in his first book of poems:

> Look! I implore, who's
> sashaying across the Bad
> Lands now—it's trepid riding
> Tate (gone loco in the
> cabeza) out of his little
> civilized element—Oh!
> It's bound to end in tears.

To write a poem out of nothing at all is Tate's genius. For him, the poem is something one did not know was there until it was written down. Image evokes image, as rhyme evokes rhyme in formal prosody, until there is a poem. The poet is like a fortune-teller with a mirror and a dictionary. He's trying to make sense and give identities to what at first appears to be the product of wild imaginings. With all his reliance on chance, Tate has a serious purpose. He's searching for a new way to write a lyric poem. Here's one from among numerous such examples, a poem seemingly about "nothing at all" from his book *The Worshipful Company of Fletchers* (1994):

The Wrong Way Home

All night a door floated down the river.
It tried to remember little incidents of pleasure
from its former life, like the time the lovers
leaned against it kissing for hours
and whispering those famous words.
Later, there were harsh words and a shoe
was thrown and the door was slammed.
Comings and goings by the thousands,
the early mornings and late nights, years, years.

O they've got big plans, they'll make a bundle.
The door was an island that swayed in its sleep.
the moon turned the doorknob just slightly,
burned its fingers and ran,
and still the door said nothing and slept.
At least that's what they like to say,
the little fishes and so on.
Far away, a bell rang, and then a shot was fired.

Memoir of the Hawk, Tate's latest collection, is a huge book of 172 prose poems, most of them no more than a page long. He has written prose poems before and scattered them throughout his books, but this huge, single-minded effort is unusual for him. For critics and poets who have difficulty accepting the idea that free verse can be poetry, prose poetry is still another hoax perpetrated by the same folks who brought us that other outrage: Modernism. It's as implausible as a dog that sings opera. That prose poetry has a long pedigree going back to Baudelaire and Rimbaud doesn't impress them much. The attraction of the form for those who fall under its spell is precisely its status as a pariah and object of ridicule. This is what Tate himself has to say on the subject:

> The prose poem has its own means of seduction. For one thing, the deceptively simple packaging: the paragraph. People generally do not run for cover when they are confronted with a paragraph or two. The paragraph says to them: I won't take much of your time, and, if you don't mind my saying so, I am not known to be arcane, obtuse, precious, or high-fallutin'. Come on in.

Like most statements about poetry made by poets, a lot of what Tate says here is only partly true. To begin with, the poems in the new book are not printed as paragraphs but look more like poems with the usual line breaks. The prosody is still that of a prose poem in that they are made up of sentences rather than of lines. These are quick little anecdotes, allegories, and fables. In fact, they are parodies of different kinds of narratives. What they undermine is our expectation that the story will come to a point. Tate does this by mixing up the real and the imaginary, the important and the trivial. Just about anything can happen next in this kind of poetry, and that is its attraction. "It's a tragic story, but that's what's so funny," he says in one poem. Some poets want the reader to be put at ease; Tate is not worried about leaving us a little dazed.

The Splendid Rainbow

The lightning woke us at about three A.M. It sounded like a war was going on out there, the drumrolls, the cannons exploding, the bomb blasts, the blinding flashes. The electricity was out. I found the flashlight and lit some candles. The roof was leaking and the rain was lashing the windows so savagely they rattled in their casings. "What are our chances of dying?" Denny asked. "Almost certain," I said. We sat on the edge of the bed and held onto one another. The lightning bolts were striking all around us. "Denny," I said, "you are very, very beautiful and I love you with all my heart." "I'll take that to my watery grave," she said, "and smile through eternity." Then we kissed and the sun came up and the rain stopped and the birds started to sing, a bit too loudly. But, what the hell, they were in love, too.

Poets like Collins collect themselves into a single persona; Tate disperses himself among his invented characters. The poem, he has said, begins with a voice in his head, some colloquial phrase that gets it going. Since his ear for nuances of speech is so acute, the temptation to inhabit other selves is just too strong for him. If it turns out to be some bumbling oaf who will lead the reader by the end of the poem into the deepest metaphysical waters, so much the better. Tate is like a cartoonist who'll turn himself into anything and anyone from a lover hiding under the bed to a flowerpot on the windowsill. He reminds me of Saul Steinberg. Uncle Sam playing the violin on a street corner while Lady Liberty beats a toy drum for a couple of dancing ants would fit comfortably in a Tate poem.

❧

As one would expect from a book this long, Tate is not able to hit the jackpot in every poem. "It wouldn't really be pushing against the limits if I knew how it was going to turn out," he says in an interview. True. The uninterrupted derailing of expectations sometimes derails the poem too. That's the risk he takes. There are too many voices, perhaps, too many stories, too many surprising turns of events to take it all easily in. Still, if America ever gets a comic epic, it will sound like this. Tate has always had a good ear for clichés. He knows that they make the world in which we live. His new book does not have a hero, but a large cast of what one may call village idiots. They say and do all kinds of foolish things as they go about their American lives, and then, when we least expect it, they surprise us with poetry.

The Eternal Ones of the Dream

I was walking down this dirt road out in the country. It was a sunny day in early fall. I looked up and saw this donkey pulling a cart coming toward me. There was no driver nor anyone leading the donkey so far as I could see. The donkey was just moping along. When we met the donkey stopped and I scratched its snout in greeting and it seemed grateful. It seemed like a very lonely donkey, but what donkey wouldn't feel alone on the road like that? And then it occurred to me to see what, if anything, was in the cart. There was only a black box, or a coffin, about two feet long and a foot wide. I started to lift the lid, but then I didn't, I couldn't. I realized that this donkey was on some woeful mission, who knows where, to the ends of the earth, so I gave him an apple, scratched his nose a last time and waved him on, little man that I was.

"One of the great marvels and mysteries of good poetry," Tate has written, "is that it can be about literally anything . . . a fleeting daydream, some overheard gossip, idle thoughts that become their own haunted labyrinth full of monsters, some lovable, others not." This is also true of Collins in his best work. Without quite realizing it we find ourselves in our imagination and in our thoughts somewhere we had not expected to be, without a clear idea of how we got there. What Charles Mingus, the great jazz bassist, said after hearing Ornette Coleman play his saxophone applies here too: He does everything wrong, but it sounds right. What I like about Tate is that he succeeds in ways for which there are a few precedents. He makes me think that anti-poetry is the best friend poetry ever had.

UNDER DISCUSSION
David Lehman, General Editor
Donald Hall, Founding Editor

Volumes in the Under Discussion series collect reviews and essays about individual poets. The series is concerned with contemporary American and English poets about whom the consensus has not yet been formed and the final vote has not been taken. Titles in the series include: